REGISTR\.... DISTRICTS

AN ALPHABETICAL LIST OF OVER 650 DISTRICTS
WITH DETAILS OF COUNTIES, SUB-DISTRICTS
AND ADJACENT DISTRICTS

Ray Wiggins

SOCIETY OF GENEALOGISTS ENTERPRISES LTD

Published by
Society of Genealogists Enterprises Limited
14 Charterhouse Buildings
Goswell Road
London EC1M 7BA
Company Number 3899591

Society of Genealogists Enterprises Limited is a wholly owned subsidiary of
Society of Genealogists, a registered charity, no 233701

First published in 1989 by J R Wiggins,
(as *St. Catherine's House Districts*)
Reprinted 1989, 1990, 1992, 1995, 2004
Second edition 1998
Third edition 2001

© J R Wiggins 1989, 1998, 2001

ISBN 1 903462 50 9

British Library Cataloguing in Publication Data
A CIP Catalogue record for this book is available from the British Library

CONTENTS

INTRODUCTION

This book was originally published by the compiler under the title *St Catherine's House Districts* at the time when all Registers of Births, Marriages and Death were located at St Catherine's House in Kingsway, London WC2B 6JP. The same districts are also used for Census returns.

The inclusion of Counties, using the Chapman County Codes, gives a general location of the District. The Sub-Districts will help one to appreciate how far the District extends and the adjacent Districts will assist in cases where a person's birth is registered in one District and the marriage or death in another.

The list of Sub-Districts at the end may at times be used in locating a Main District or, alternatively, it will be helpful in cases where a Sub-District later became a Main District.

To keep the list as short as possible Sub-Districts which are obviously a parish of a large town, or include the name of the Main District, are generally omitted. Likewise, Districts in the Isle of Man and the Channel Islands are not included.

Included at the end of the Introduction are the Registration District Volume Numbers for each County with the periods to which they refer.

Ray Wiggins. 1998

POST AUTHOR'S NOTE:

The indexes are now available for public consultation at the Family Records Centre, Myddelton Place, 1 Myddelton Street, London EC14 1UW. Fiche copies can be found at various record offices and information from the indexes is also located on various websites.

CHAPMAN COUNTY CODES

AGY	Anglesey	LEI	Leicestershire
BDF	Bedfordshire	LIN	Lincolnshire
BKM	Buckinghamshire	LND	London
BRE	Breconshire	MDX	Middlesex
BRK	Berkshire	MER	Merionethshire
CAE	Caenarvonshire	MGY	Montgomeryshire
CAM	Cambridgeshire	MON	Monmouthshire
CGN	Cardiganshire	NBL	Northumberland
CHS	Cheshire	NFK	Norfolk
CMN	Carmarthenshire	NTH	Northamptonshire
CON	Cornwall	NTT	Nottinghamshire
CUL	Cumberland	OXF	Oxfordshire
DBY	Derbyshire	PEM	Pembrokeshire
DEN	Denbighshire	RAD	Radnorshire
DEV	Devonshire	RUT	Rutland
DOR	Dorset	SAL	Shropshire
DUR	Durham	SFK	Suffolk
ESS	Essex	SOM	Somerset
FLN	Flint	SRY	Surrey
GLA	Glamorganshire	SSX	Sussex
GLS	Gloucestershire	STS	Staffordshire
HAM	Hampshire	WAR	Warwickshire
HEF	Herefordshire	WES	Westmorland
HRT	Hertfordshire	WIL	Wiltshire
HUN	Huntingdonshire	WOR	Worcestershire
KEN	Kent	YKS	Yorkshire
LAN	Lancashire		

REGISTRATION DISTRICT VOLUME NUMBERS

	1837-1852	1852-1946	1946-1974	1974-Date
Greater London	1-5	1A-ID	5A-5D	11-15
Surrey	4	2A	5F	11,13,14,17
Kent	5	2A	5F	11,16
Sussex	7	2B	5H	18
Hampshire	7,8	2C	6B	14,20,23
Berkshire	6	2C	6A	19,20
Hertfordshire	6	3A	4B	10,11
Oxfordshire	16	3A	6A	20
Buckinghamshire	16	3A	6B	19
Middlesex	3	3A	5A-5E	12,13
Cambridgeshire/Bedfordshire	6,14	3B	4A	9
Huntingtonshire	14	3B	4B	9
Northhamptonshire	15	3B	3B	7
Essex	12	4A	4A	9,11,13
Suffolk	12,13	4A	4B	10,11
Norfolk	13	4B	4B	10
Wiltshire	8	5A	7C	23
Dorset/Somerset	10	5C	7C	22,23
Devon/Cornwall/Scilly	9	5B-5C	7A	21
Gloucestershire	11	6A	7B	22
Shropshire	18	6A	9A	30
Herefordshire	26	6A	9A	29
Staffordshire	17	6B	9B	30,34
Worcestershire	18	6C	9D	29,33
Warwickshire	16	6D	9C	31,32,33,34
Leicestershire	15	7A	3A	6
Lincolnshire	14	7A	3B	7
Rutlandshire	14,15	7A	3C	6
Nottinghamshire	15	7B	3C	6,8
Derbyshire	19	7B	3A	6
Cheshire	19	8A	10A	35,37,39
Lancashire	20,21	8B-8E	10B-10F	1,35-40
Yorkshire	22,23,24	9A-9D	1B,2A-2D	2,3,4,5,7
Durham	24	10A	1A	1,2
Cumberland	25	10B	1A	1
Northumberland/Westmorland	25	10B	1B	1,2
Wales 24,25,26,27,28	26,27	11A,11B	8A-8C	
Isle of Wight	-	2B	6B	20

MAIN DISTRICTS

MAIN DISTRICT (Sub-Districts)
Adjacent Districts

ABERAYRON, CGN. (Llandisilio, Llansaintffraid)
Aberystwyth, Lampeter, Newcastle-in-Emlyn, Tregaron

ABERGAVENNY, MON. (Blaenavon, Llanarth, Llanvilhangel)
Bedwellty, Crickhowell, Hay, Hereford, Monmouth, Pontypool

ABERYSTWYTH, CGN. (Geneurglynn, Llanrhystyd, Rheidol)
Aberayron, Machynlleth, Newtown, Rhayader, Tregaron

ABINGDON, BRK. (Cumnor, Fyfield, Nuneham Courtney, Sutton Courtney)
Faringdon, Headington, Oxford, Thame, Wallingford, Wantage, Witney, Woodstock

ALCESTER, WAR. (Bidford, Feckenham, Studley)
Droitwich, Evesham, Kings Norton, Pershore, Stratford-on-Avon

ALDERBURY, WIL. (Britford, Downton)
Amesbury, Fordingbridge, New Forest, Romsey, Salisbury, Stockbridge, Wilton

ALNWICK, NBL. (Embleton, Warkworth)
Belford, Glendale, Morpeth, Rothbury

ALRESFORD, HAM. (Ropley)
Alton, Basingstoke, Droxford, Petersfield, Winchester

ALSTON, CUL.
Haltwhistle, Hexham, Penrith, Teesdale, Weardale

ALTON, HAM. (Binsted)
Alresford, Basingstoke, Farnham, Hartley Wintney, Midhurst, Petersfield

ALTRINCHAM, CHS. (Knutsford, Lymm, Wilmslow)
Barton-upon-Irwell, Chorlton, Macclesfield, Northwich, Runcorn, Stockport, Warrington

ALVERSTOKE, HAM.
Fareham, Portsea Island

AMERSHAM, BKM. (Beaconsfield, Chalfont, Chesham, Missenden)
Aylesbury, Berhamstead, Eton, Hemel Hempstead, Watford, Wycombe

AMESBURY, WIL. (Orcheston, Winterbourne)
Alderbury, Andover, Devizes, Pewsey, Stockbridge, Warminster, Wilton

AMPTHILL, BDF. (Cranfield, Shillingford)
Bedford, Biggleswade, Hitchin, Luton, Newport Pagnell, Woburn

ANDOVER, HAM. (Amport, Hurstbourne-Tarrant, Longparish, Ludgershall)
Amesbury, Hungerford, Kingsclere, Pewsey, Stockbridge, Whitchurch, Winchester

ANGLESEY (Amlwch, Bryngwan, Holyhead, Llanddausaint, Llandyfrydog, Llangefni)
Bangor, Carnarvon

ASHBORNE, DBY. (Brailsford, Brassington, Calton, Hartington, Mayfield
Bakewell, Belper, Burton-upon-Trent, Cheadle, Leek, Uttoxeter

ASHBY-DE-LA-ZOUCH, LEI. (Hartshorn, Measham, Whitwick)
Burton-upon-Trent, Lichfield, Loughborough, Market Harborough, Shardlow, Tamworth

ASHTON-UNDER-LYNE, LAN. (Audenshaw, Denton, Duckinfield, Hartshead, Knotts Lanes, Mottram, Newton, Stayley)
Chorlton, Hayfield, Huddersfield, Manchester, Oldham, Saddleworth, Stockport, Wortley

ASKRIGG, YKS. (Hawes)
East Ward, Leyburn, Reeth, Sedburgh, Settle

ASTON, WAR. (Deritend, Duddeston, Erdington, Sutton Coldfield)
Birmingham, Burton-upon-Trent, Kings Norton, Lichfield, Meriden, Solihull, Tamworth

ATCHAM, SAL. (Alberbury, Battlefield, Condover, Montford, Pontersbury, Westbury)
Church Stretton, Clun, Ellesmere, Llanfyllin, Madeley, Montgomery, Oswestry, Shrewsbury, Wellington, Wem

ATHERSTONE, WAR.
Hinckley, Nuneaton, Market Bosworth, Meriden, Tamworth

AUCKLAND, DUR. (Bishop Auckland, Hamsterley)
Darlington, Durham, Stockton, Teesdale, Weardale

AXBRIDGE, SOM. (Banwell, Blagdon, Burnham, Wedmore)
Bedminster, Bridgwater, Clutton, Wells

AXMINSTER, DEV. (Chardstock, Colyton, Lyme)
Beaminster, Bridport, Chard, Honiton

AYLESBURY, BKM. (Aston Clinton, Haddenham, Waddesdon)
Amersham, Berkhamstead, Bicester, Buckingham, Leighton Buzzard, Winslow, Wycombe, Thame

AYLSHAM, NFK. (Buxton, Eynsford)
Erpingham, Mitford, St Faiths, Tunstead, Walsingham

BAKEWELL, DBY. (Matlock, Tideswell)
Ashborne, Belper, Chapel-en-le-Frith, Chesterfield, Ecclesall Bierlow,Leek, Macclesfield, Wortley

BALA, MER.
Corwen, Dolgelly, Festiniog, Llanfyllin, Llanrwst

BANBURY, OXF. (Bloxham, Chopredy, Swalcliffe)
Brackley, Chipping Norton, Daventry, Shipston-on-Stour, Southam, Woodstock

BANGOR, CAE. (Beaumaris, Llanllechid)
Anglesey, Carnarvon, Conway, Festiniog, Llanrwst

BARNET, MDX. (Finchley, South Mimms)
Edmonton, Hampstead, Hatfield, Hendon, Pancras, St Albans, Watford

BARNSLEY, YKS. (Darfield, Darton, Worsbrough)
Dewsbury, Doncaster, Hemsworth, Rotherham, Wakefield, Wortley

BARNSTAPLE, DEV. (Bishops Tawton, Braunton, Combmartin, Ilfracombe, Paracombe)
Bideford, Dulverton, South Molton, Torrington, Williton

BARROW-IN-FURNESS, LAN. - previously part of Ulverston

BARROW-UPON-SOAR, LEI. (Querndon, Rothley, Whitwick)
Billesdon, Blaby, Leicester, Loughborough, Market Harborough, Melton Mowbray

BARTON-UPON-IRWELL, LAN. (Stretford, Worsley)
Altrincham, Chorlton, Leigh, Salford, Warrington

BARTON REGIS, GLS. - previously known as Clifton

BASFORD, NTT. (Arnold, Bulwell, Carlton, Greaseley, Ilkeston, Wilford)
Belper, Bingham, Loughborough, Mansfield, Nottingham, Radford, Shardlow, Southwell

BASINGSTOKE, HAM. (Bramley, Dummer)
Alresford, Alton, Bradfield, Hartley Wintney, Kingsclere, Whitchurch, Winchester

BATH, SOM. (Abbey, Batheaston, Bathwick, Lansdown, Lyncombe, Twerton, Walcot)
Bradford-on-Avon, Chippenham, Chipping Sodbury, Clutton, Frome, Keynsham

BATTLE, SSX. (Bexhill, Ewhurst)
Cranbrook, Eastbourne, Hailsham, Hastings, Rye, Ticehurst

BEAMINSTER, DOR. (Evershot, Misterton, Netherbury)
Axminster, Bridport, Chard, Dorchester, Sherborne, Yeovil

BEDALE, YKS. (Masham)
Leyburn, Northallerton, Richmond, Ripon, Thirsk

BEDFORD (Cardington, Harrold, Kempston, Riseley, Sharnbrook, Turvey)
Ampthill, Biggleswade, Newport Pagnell, St Neots, Wellingborough

BEDMINSTER, SOM. (Long Ashton, St George, Yatton)
Axbridge, Bristol, Clifton, Clutton, Keynsham

BEDWELLTY, MON. (Aberystruth, Rock, Tredegar)
Abergavenny, Crickhowell, Merthyr Tydfil, Newport, Pontypool

BELFORD, NBL.
Alnwick, Berwick, Glendale

BELLINGHAM, NBL. (Kirkwhelpington)
Castle Ward, Brampton, Haltwhistle, Hexham, Longtown, Morprth, Rothbury

BELPER, DBY. (Alfreton, Duffield, Horsley, Ripley, Wirksworth)
Ashborne, Bakewell, Basford, Burton-upon-Trent, Derby, Chesterfield, Mansfield

BERKHAMSTEAD, HRT. (Tring)
Amersham, Aylesbury, Hemel Hempstead, Leighton Buzzard, Luton

BERMONDSEY, LND.
Newington, Rotherhithe, St George Southwark, St Olave, St Saviour

BERWICK, NBL. (Islelandshire, Norhamshire)
Belford, Glendale

BETHNAL GREEN, LND.
Hackney, Mile End Old Town, Shoreditch, West Ham

BEVERLEY, YKS. (Leven, Lockington, South Cave)
Driffield, Goole, Howden, Hull, Pocklington, Skirlaugh

BICESTER, OXF. (Bletchington)
Aylesbury, Banbury, Brackley, Buckingham, Headington, Wodstock

BIDEFORD, DEV. (Bradworthy, Hartland, Milton Damerel, Northam, Parkham)
Barnstaple, Holsworthy, Torrington

BIGGLESWADE, BDF. (Potton)
Apthill, Bedford, Caxton, Hitchin, Royston, St Neots

BILLERICAY, ESS. (Brentwood, Great Burstead, Wickford)
Chelmsford, Ongar, Orsett, Rochford, Romford

BILLESDON, LEI.
Barrow-upon-Soar, Blaby, Leicester, Lutterworth, Market Harborough, Melton Mowbray, Oakham, Uppingham

BINGHAM, NTT. (Ratcliffe-on-Trent)
Basford, Loughborough, Melton Mowbray, Newark, Radford, Shardlow, Southwell

BIRKENHEAD, CHS. (Tranmere, Wallasey)
Liverpool, West Derby, Wirral

BIRMINGHAM, WAR.
Aston, Kings Norton, Solihull, West Bromwich

BISHOP STORTFORD, HRT. (Braughing, Stansted, Sunbridgeworth)
Dunmow, Epping, Royston, Saffron Walden, Ware

BLABY, LEI. (Enderby, Wigston)
Barrow-upon- Soar, Billesdon, Hinckley, Leicester, Lutterworth, Market Bosworth, Market Harborough

BLACKBURN, LAN. (Billington, Darwen, Harwood, Mellor, Oswaldtwistle, Wilton)
Bolton, Burnley, Chorley, Clitheroe, Haslingden, Preston

BLANDFORD, DOR. (Milton Abbas)
Dorchester, Shaftesbury, Sturminster, Tisbury, Wareham, Wimborne

BLEAN, KEN. (Herne, Sturry, Whitstable)
Bridge, Eastry, Faversham, Thanet

BLOFIELD, NFK. (South Walsham)
Flegg, Henstead, Loddon, Mutford, St Faiths, Tunstead, Yarmouth

BLYTHING, SFK. (Halesworth, Wenhaston, Westleton)
Hoxne, Mutford, Plomesgate, Wangford

BODMIN, CON. (Egloshayle, Lanlivery, St Mabin)
Camelford, Liskeard, St Austell, St Columb

BOLTON, LAN. (Edgeworth, Farnworth, Halliwell, Horwich, Hulton, Lever, Sharples, Tongwith Haulgh, Turton, West Houghton)
Blackburn, Bury, Chorley, Haslingden, Leigh, Manchester, Salford, Wigan

BOOTLE, CUL. (Muncaster)
Cockermouth, Kendal, Ulverston, Whitehaven

BOSMERE, SFK. (Coddenham, Needham Market)
Cosford, Hartismere, Hoxne, Plomesgate, Samford, Stow, Woodbridge

BOSTON, LIN. (Bennington, Kirton-in-Holland, Sibsey, Swineshead)
Holbeach, Horncastle, Sleaford, Spalding, Spilsby

BOURNE LIN. (Aslackby, Corby, Deeping)
Grantham, Oakham, Peterborough, Sleaford, Spalding, Stamford

BRACKLEY, NTH. (Sulgrave)
Banbury, Bicester, Buckingham, Daventry, Newport Pagnell, Towcester, Woodstock

BRADFIELD, BRK. (Bucklebury, Mortimer, Tilehurst)
Basingstoke, Hartley, Wintney, Henley, Kingsclere, Newbury, Reading, Wallingford, Wantage, Wokingham

BRADFORD-ON-AVON, WIL.
Bath, Calne, Chippenham, Clutton, Devizes, Melksham, Westbury

BRADFORD, YKS. (Bowling, Calverley, Cleckheaton, Driglington, Horton, Idle, North Bierley, Pudsey, Shipley, Thornton, Wilsden)
Dewsbury, Guiseley, Halifax, Huddersfield, Keighley, Leeds, Otley,Rothwell, Wharfedale

BRAINTREE, ESS. (Bocking, Finchingfield)
Chelmsford, Dunmow, Halstead, Risbridge, Witham, Saffron Walden

BRAMLEY, YKS. (Gildersome) - previously part of Hunslet and Wortley

BRAMPTON, CUL. (Hayton, Walton)
Bellingham, Carlisle, Haltwhistle, Longtown, Penrith

BRECKNOCK, BRE. (Devynnock, Llangorse, Merthyr Cynog, Penkelly)
Builth, Crickhowell, Hay, Llandovery, Merthyr Tydfil, Neath

BRENTFORD, MDX. (Acton, Chiswick, Isleworth, Twickenham)
Hendon, Kensington, Kingston, Richmond, Staines, Uxbridge, Wandsworth

BRIDGE, KEN. (Barham, Chartham)
Dover, East Ashford, Eastry, Elham, Faversham, Thanet

BRIDGEND, GLA. (Cowbridge, Maesteg)
Cardiff, Merthyr Tydfil, Neath

BRIDGWATER, SOM. (Huntspill, Middlezoy, North Petherton, Polden Hill, Stowey)
Axbridge, Langport, Taunton, Wells, Williton

BRIDGNORTH, SAL. (Chetton, Worfield)
Church Stretton, Cleobury Mortimer, Kidderminster, Ludlow, Madeley, Shifnal, Stourbridge, Tenbury, Wolverhampton

BRIDLINGTON, YKS. (Hunmanby, Skipsea)
Driffield, Scarborough, Skirlaugh

BRIDPORT, DOR. (Burton Bradstock, Whitchurch Canonicorum)
Axminster, Bedminster, Dorchester, Weymouth

BRIGHTON, SSX.
Cuckfield, Lewes, Steyning, Worthing

BRISTOL, GLS.
Bedminster, Clifton, Clutton, Keynsham

BRIXWORTH, NTH. (Moulton, Spratton)
Daventry, Kettering, Lutterworth, Market Harborough, Northampton, Rugby, Wellingborough

BROMLEY, KEN. (Chislehurst)
Battersea, Croydon, Dartford, Godstone, Lewisham, Sevenoaks

BROMSGROVE, WOR. (Belbroughton, Tardebigg)
Alcester, Droitwich, Kidderminster, Kings Norton, Stourbridge

BROMYARD, HEF. (Bishops Frome, Brockhampton)
Hereford, Leominster, Ledbury, Martley, Tenbury, Upton-upon-Severn

BUCKINGHAM, BKM. (Leckhampstead, Tingewick)
Aylesbury, Bicester, Brackley, Potterspury, Towcester, Winslow

BUILTH, BRE. (Abergwessin, Colwyn)
Brecknock, Hay, Llandovery, Presteigne, Rhayader, Tregaron

BURNLEY, LAN. (Colne, Padiham, Pendle)
Blackburn, Clitheroe, Haslingden, Keighley, Rochdale, Skipton, Todmorden

BURTON-UPON-TRENT, STS. (Gresley, Repton, Tutbury)
Ashborne, Ashby-de-la-Zouch, Belper, Lichfield, Shardlow, Uttoxeter

BURY, LAN. (Birtle, Elton, Heywood, Holcombe, Pilkington, Radcliffe,
Tottington, Lower End, Walmersley)
Bolton, Haslingden, Manchester, Oldham, Rochdale

BURY ST EDMUNDS, SFK.
Thingoe

CAISTOR, LIN. (Great Grimsby, Market Rasen)
Gainsborough, Glanford Brigg, Horncastle, Lincoln, Louth

CALNE, WIL.
Chippenham, Cricklade, Devizes, Malmesbury, Marlborough, Melksham

CAMBERWELL, LND. (Dulwich, Peckham, St George)
Lambeth, Lewisham, Newington, Rotherhithe

CAMBRIDGE, CAM.
Chesteton

CAMELFORD, CON. (Boscastle)
Bodmin, Launceston, Liskeard, Stratton

CANNOCK, STS. - previously known as Penkridge

CANTERBURY, KEN.
Blean, Bridge

CARDIFF, GLA. (Caerphilly, Llantrisaint, St Nicholas, Whitchurch)
Bridgend, Merthyr Tydfil, Neath, Newport

CARDIGAN, CGN. (Llandygwydd, Newport)
Carmarthen, Haverfordwest, Narberth, Newcastle-in-Emlyn

CARLISLE, CUL. (Burgh, Dalston, Stanwix, Wetheral)
Brampton, Longtown, Penrith, Wigton

CARMARTHEN, CMN. (Clears, Conwil, Llangendeirne)
Cardigan, Llanelly, Llandilowfawr, Narberth, Newcastle-in-Emlyn

CARNARVON, CAE (Llandwrog, Llanidan, Llanrug)
Anglesey, Bangor, Festiniog, Llanrwst, Pwllheli

CASTLE WARD, NBL. (Ponteland, Stamfordham)
Bellingham, Gateshead, Hexham, Morpeth, Newcastle-upon-Tyne, Tynemouth

CATHERINGTON, HAM. (Horndean)
Droxford, Fareham, Havant, Petersfield, Westbourne

CAXTON, CAM.
Chesterton, Huntingdon, Royston, St Ives, St Neots

CHARD, SOM. (Combe St Nicholas, Crewkerne, Ilminster)
Axminster, Beaminster, Langport, Taunton, Yeovil

CHAPEL-EN-LE-FRITH, DBY. (Buxton)
Bakewell, Hayfield, Macclesfield, Stockport, Wortley

CHEADLE, STS. (Alton, Dilhorne, Ipstones)
Ashborne, Leak, Stoke-upon-Trent, Stone, Uttoxeter

CHELMSFORD, ESS. (Great Baddow, Great Waltham, Ingatestone, Writtle)
Billericay, Braintree, Dunmow, Maldon, Ongar, Rochford, Witham

CHELSEA, MDX.
Kensington, St George Hanover Square, St James Westminster, Westminster

CHELTENHAM, GLS. (Charlton Kings)
Cirencester, Gloucester, Northleach, Stroud, Tewkesbury, Winchcomb

CHEPSTOW, MON. (Lydney, Shire Newton)
Monmouth, Newport, Pontypool, Thornbury, Westbury-on-Severn

CHERTSEY, SRY. (Chobham, Walton)
Easthampstead, Epsom, Farnborough, Guildford, Kingston, Staines, Windsor

CHESTER, CHS - previously known as Great Boughton

CHESTERFIELD, DBY. (Ashover, Bolsover, Dronfield, Eckington)
Bakewell, Belper, Ecclesall Bierlow, Mansfield, Rotherham, Sheffield, Worksop

CHESTER-LE-STREET, DUR. (Harraton)
Durham, Gateshead, Houghton-le-Spring, South Shields, Sunderland

CHESTERTON, CAM. (Fulbourn, Great Shelford, Willingham)
Cambridge, Caxton, Ely, Linton, Newmarket, Royston, St Ives

CHICHESTER, SSX. (South Bersted, Sutton)
Midhurst, Petworth, Thakeham, Westbourne, Westhampnett, Worthing

CHIPPENHAM, WIL. (Castle Combe, Christian Malford, Corsham)
Bath, Bradford-on-Avon, Calne, Chipping Sodbury, Devizes, Malmesbury, Melksham

CHIPPING NORTON, OXF. (Charlbury)
Banbury, Shipston-on-Stour, Stow on the Wold, Witney, Woodstock

CHIPPING SODBURY, GLS. (Hawkesbury, Iron Acton, Marshfield)
Bath, Chippenham, Clifton, Dursley, Keynsham, Malmesbury, Tethbury, Thornbury

CHORLEY, LAN. (Brindle, Croston, Leyland, Rivington)
Blackburn, Bolton, Ormskirk, Preston, Wigan

CHORLTON, LAN. (Ardwick, Didsbury, Hulme)
Altrincham, Ashton-under-Lyne, Barton-upon-Irwell, Manchester, Salford, Stockport

CHRISTCHURCH, HAM.
Lymington, New Forest, Poole, Ringwood, Wimborne

CHURCH STRETTON, SAL. (Wall)
Atcham, Bridgnorth, Clun, Ludlow, Madeley

CIRENCESTER, GLS. (Cotswold, Fairford)
Cheltenham, Cricklade, Faringdon, Highworth, Malmesbury, Northleach, Stroud, Tetbury

CLEOBURY MORTIMER, SAL. (Stottesden)
Bridgnorth, Kidderminster, Ludlow, Tenbury

CLERKENWELL, LND. (Anwell, Goswell Street, Pentonville, St James)
Holborn, Islington, London City, St Luke

CLIFTON, GLS. (Ashley, Stapleton, Westbury)
Bedminster, Bristol, Chipping Sodbury, Clutton, Keynsham, Thornbury

CLITHEROE, LAN. (Chipping, Gisburn, Slaidburn, Whalley)
Blackburn, Burnley, Lancaster, Preston, Settle, Skipton

CLUN, SAL. (Bishops Castle, Norbury, North Lydbury)
Atcham, Church Stretton, Ludlow, Knighton, Montgomery, Newtown

CLUTTON, SOM. (Chew Magna, Harptree, Midsomer Norton)
Axbridge, Bath, Bedminster, Bristol, Frome, Keynsham, Shepton Mallet, Wells

COCKERMOUTH, CUL. (Keswick, Maryport, Workington)
Bootle, Kendal, Penrith, West Ward, Whitehaven, Wigton

COLCHESTER, ESS.
Lexden, Tendring

CONGLETON, CHS. (Church Hulme, Sandbach)
Altrincam, Leek, Macclesfield, Nantwich, Northwich, Wolstanton

CONWAY, CAE. (Creuddyn, Llechwedd-Isarf)
Bangor, Llanrwst, St Asaph

COOKHAM, BRK. (Bray)
Easthampstead, Eton, Windsor, Wokingham, Wycombe

CORWEN, MER. (Gwyddelwern, Llangollen)
Bala, Ellesmere, Llanfyllin, Oswestry, Ruthin, Wrexham

COSFORD, SFK. (Hadleigh, Lavenham)
Bosmere, Samford, Stow, Sudbury, Thingoe

COVENTRY, WAR.
Foleshill, Meriden, Nuneaton, Rugby, Warwick

CRANBROOK, KEN. (Hawkhurst)
Hollingbourn, Maidstone, Tenterden, Tunbridge, West Ashford

CREDITON, DEV. (Bow, Cheriton, Fitzpaine, Morchard Bishop)
Newton Abbot, Okehampton, St Thomas, South Molton, Tiverton, Torrington

CRICKLADE, WIL. (Wootton-Bassett)
Calne, Cirencester, Highworth, Malmesbury, Marlborough

CRICKHOWELL, BRE. (Cwmdu, Llanelly, Llangattock, Llangunider)
Abergavenny, Bedwellty, Brecknock, Hay, Merthyr Tydfil

CROYDON, SRY. (Mitcham)
Battersea, Bromley, Camberwell, Epsom, Godstone, Kingston, Lambeth, Lewisham, Reigate, Wandsworth

CUCKFIELD, SSX. (Hurstpierpoint, Lindfield)
Brighton, East Grinstead, Horsham, Lewes, Steyning, Uckfield

DARLINGTON, DUR. (Aycliffe)
Auckland, Northallerton, Richmond, Stockton, Teesdale

DARTFORD, KEN. (Bexley, Farningham)
Battle, Bromley, Lewisham, Malling, North Aylesford, Rye, Sevenoaks, Ticehurst

DAVENTRY, NTH. (Long Buckby, Weedon)
Banbury, Brackley, Brixworth, Northampton, Rugby, Southam, Towester

DEPWADE, NFK. (Diss, Forncett, Harleston, Stratton)
Forehoe, Guiltcross, Hartismere, Henstead, Hoxne, Loddon, Wangford, Wayland

DERBY, DBY.
Belper, Burton-upon-Trent, Shardlow

DEVIZES, WIL. (Bishops Canning, Bromham, Lavington)
Amesbury, Calne, Chippenham, Marlborough, Pewsey, Warminster, Westbury

DEWSBURY, YKS. (Batley, Gomersal, Liversedge, Mirfield, Morley, Ossett, Soothill, Thornhill)
Barnsley, Bradford, Halifax, Huddersfield, Rothwell, Wakefield, Wortley

DOCKING, NFK. (Burnham, Snettisham)
Freebridge Lynn, Mitford, Walsingham

DOLGELLY, MER. (Barmouth, Tallyllyn)
Bala, Festiniog, Llanfyllin, Machynlleth

DONCASTER, YKS. (Barmborough, Bawtry, Campsall, Tickhill)
Barnsley, East Tetford, Hemsworth, Goole, Pontefract, Rotherham, Thorne, Worksop

DORCHESTER, DOR. (Cerne, Maiden Newton, Puddletown)
Beaminster, Blandford, Bridport, Sherborne, Sturminster, Wareham, Weymouth

DORKING, SRY. (Capel)
Epsom, Guildford, Hambledon, Horsham, Petworth, Reigate

DOVER, KEN. (Houghton)
Eastry, Elham, Bridge

DOWNHAM, NFK. (Fincham, Wiggenhall)
Ely, Freebridge Lynn, Kings Lynn, Swaffham, Thetford, Wisbech

DRIFFIELD, YKS. (Bainton, Foston, Langtoft)
Beverley, Bridlington, Malton, Pocklington, Scarborough, Skirlaugh

DROITWICH, WOR. (Claines, Ombersley)
Alcester, Birmingham, Kidderminster, Martley, Pershore, Upton-upon-Severn, Worcester

DROXFORD, HAM. (Bishops Waltham, Hambledon, West Meon)
Alresford, Catherington, Fareham, Havant, Petersfield, South Stoneham, Winchester

DUDLEY, STS. (Rowley Regis, Sedgley, Tipton)
Stourbridge, Walsall, West Bromwich, Wolverhampton

DULVERTON, SOM.
Barnstaple, South Molton, Tiverton, Wellington, Williton

DUNMOW, ESS. (Hatfield, Stebbing, Thaxted)
Bishop Stortford, Braintree, Chelmsford, Epping, Ongar, Saffron Walden

DURHAM, DUR. (Lanchester, St Nicholas, St Oswald, Tanfield)
Auckland, Chester-le-Street, Easington, Gateshead, Hartlepool, Hexham, Houghton-le-Spring, Stockton, Weardale

DURSLEY, GLS. (Uley, Wotton-under-Edge)
Chipping Sodbury, Stroud, Tetbury, Thornbury, Westbury-on-Severn, Wheatenhurst

EASINGTON, DUR.
Durham, Hartlepool, Houghton-le-Spring, Stockton, Sunderland

EASINGWOLD, YKS. (Coxwold, Stillington)
Great Ouseburn, Helmsley, Malton, Ripon, Thirsk, York

EAST ASHFORD, KEN. (Aldington, Brabourne, Wye)
Bridge, Elham, Faversham, Romney Marsh, Rye, Tenterden, West Ashford

EASTBOURNE, SSX. (Westham)
Battle, Hailsham, Lewes

EAST GRINSTEAD, SSX. (Withyham, Worth)
Cuckfield, Lewes, Godstone, Reigate, Ticehurst, Tunbridge, Uckfield

EASTHAMPSTEAD, BRK. (Bracknell)
Chertsey, Cookham, Farnborough, Windsor, Wokingham

EAST LONDON, LND.
London City, Whitechapel

EAST PRESTON, SSX. - previously known as Worthing

EAST RETFORD, NTT . (Clarborough, Gringley, Tuxford)
Doncaster, Gainsborough, Newark, Southwell, Worksop

EASTRY, KEN. (Deal, Eythorn, Sandwich, Wingham)
Blean, Bridge, Dover, Elham, Thanet

EAST STONEHOUSE, DEV.
Plymouth, Plympton St Mary, Stoke Damerel

EAST WARD, WES. (Appleby, Kirkby, Stephen Orton)
Alston, Askrigg, Kendal, Penrith, Reeth, Sedburgh, Teesdale, West Ward

ECCLESALL BIERLOW, YKS. (Nether Hallam, Norton, Upper Hallam)
Bakewell, Chesterfield, Rotherham, Sheffield, Wortley

EDMONTON, MDX. (Cheshunt, Enfield, Hornsey, Tottenham, Waltham Abbey)
Barnet, Epping, Hackney, Hatfield, Islington, Pancras, West Ham

ELHAM, KEN. (Folkestone, Hythe)
Bridge, Dover, East Ashford, Eastry, Romney Marsh

ELLESMERE, SAL. (Baschurch, Hanmer, Overton)
Atcham, Nantwich, Oswestry, Wem, Whitchurch, Wrexham

ELY, CAM. (Haddenham, Littleport, Sutton)
Chesterton, Downham, Mildenhall, Newmarket, North Witchford, St Ives, Thetford

EPPING, ESS. (Chigwell, Harlow)
Bishop Stortford, Dunmow, Edmonton, Ongar, Romford, Ware, West Ham

EPSOM, SRY. (Carshalton, Leatherhead)
Chertsey, Croydon, Dorking, Guildford, Kingston, Reigate

ERPINGHAM, NFK. (Cromer, Holt, North Walsham)
Aylsham, Tunstead, Walsingham

ETON, BKM. (Burnham, Iver)
Amersham, Cookham, Staines, Uxbridge, Watford, Windsor, Wycombe

EVESHAM, WOR. (Broadway)
Alcester, Pershore, Shipston-on-Stour, Stratford-on-Avon, Winchcomb

EXETER, DEV.
St Thomas

FALMOUTH, CON. (Constantine, Mylor, Penryn)
Helston, Redruth, Truro

FAREHAM, HAM. (Titchfield)
Alverstoke, Catherington, Droxford, Havant, Isle of Wight, New Forest, Portsea Island, South Stoneham

FARINGDON, BRK. (Buckland, Shrivenham)
Abingdon, Highworth, Hungerford, Wantage, Witney

FARNBOROUGH, HAM. (Headley)
Chertsey, Easthamstead, Farnham, Guildford, Hambledon, Hartley Wintney, Wokingham

FARNHAM, SRY. (Frimley)
Alton, Farnborough, Hambledon, Hartley Wintney, Midhurst

FAVERSHAM, KEN. (Boughton, Teynham)
Blean, Bridge, East Ashford, Hollingbourn, Milton, Sheppey, West Ashford

FESTINIOG, MER. (Llanfihangelytraethau, Tremadoc)
Bala, Bangor, Carnarvon, Dolgelly, Llanrwst, Pwllheli

FLEGG, NFK.
Blofield, Loddon, Mutford, Tunstead, Yarmouth

FOLESHILL, WAR. (Sowe)
Coventry, Hinckley, Lutterworth, Meriden, Nuneaton, Rugby

FORDEN, MGY. - previously known as Montgomery

FORDINGBRIDGE, HAM.
Alderbury, New Forest, Ringwood, Wimborne

FOREHOE, NFK. (Costessey, Wymondham)
Depwade, Guiltcross, Henstead, Mitford, Norwich, St Faiths, Wayland

FREEBRIDGE LYNN, NFK. (Castle Riding, Gayton, Hillington, Middleton)
Docking, Downham, Kings Lynn, Mitford, Swaffham, Walsingham, Wisbech

FROME, SOM. (Kilmersdon, Nunney, Road)
Bath, Bradford-on-Avon, Clutton, Mere, Shepton Mallet, Warminster, Westbury, Wincanton

FYLDE, LAN. (Kirkham, Lytham, Poulton-le-Fylde)
Garstang, Ormskirk, Preston

GAINSBOROUGH, LIN. (Marton, Misterton, Owston, Scotter, Willingham)
Caistor, Doncaster, Glanford Brigg, Lincoln, Newark, Thorne

GARSTANG, LAN. (St Michael-on-Wyre, Stalmine)
Fylde, Lancaster, Preston

GATESHEAD, DUR. (Heworth, Whickham, Winlaton)
*Castle Ward, Chester-le-Street, Durham, Hexham, Newcastle-upon-Tyne,
South Shields, Sunderland, Tynemouth*

GLANFORD BRIGG, LIN. (Barton, Brigg, Winterton)
Caistor, Gainsborough, Goole, Thorne

GLENDALE, NBL. (Ford, Wooler)
Alnwick, Belford, Berwick, Rothbury

GLOUCESTER (Kingsholm, South Hamlet)
Cheltenham, Newent, Stroud, Tewkesbury, Westbury-on-Severn, Wheatenhurst

GODSTONE, SRY.
Bromley, Croydon, East Grinstead, Reigate, Sevenoaks

GOOLE, YKS. (Snaith, Swinefleet)
Doncaster, Glanford Brigg, Howden, Pontefract, Selby, Thorne

GOWER, GLA.
Llanelly, Swansea

GRANTHAM, LIN. (Colsterworth, Denton)
Bourne, Melton Mowbray, Newark, Oakham, Sleaford

GRAVESEND, KEN.
North Aylesford

GREAT BOUGHTON, CHS. (Chester, Hawarden,Tattenhall)
*Ellesmere, Holywell, Nantwich, Northwich, Runcorn, Whitchurch, Wirral,
Wrexham*

GREAT OUSEBURN, YKS. (Boroughbridge, Poppleton, Whixley)
Easingwold, Kirk Deighton, Knaresborough, Ripon, Tadcaster, York

GREENWICH, LND. (Deptford, Woolwich)
Camberwell, Lewisham, Rotherhithe

GUILDFORD, SRY. (Albury, Godalming, Ripley, Woking)
Chertsey, Dorking, Epsom, Farnborough, Farnham, Hambledon

GUILTCROSS, NFK. (Banham, Kenninghall)
Depwade, Forehoe, Hartismere, Stow, Thingoe, Wayland

GUISBOROUGH, YKS. (Danby, Kirk-Leatham, Lofthouse, Marske)
Helmsley, Pickering, Stockton, Stokesley, Whitby

HACKNEY, LND. (Stamford Hill, Stoke Newington)
Bethnal Green, Islington, Shoreditch, West Ham

HAILSHAM, SSX. (Hellingly)
Battle, Eastbourne, Lewes, Ticehurst, Uckfield

HALIFAX, YKS. (Brighouse, Elland, Luddenham, Northowram, Ovendon, Rastrick, Ripponden, Southowram, Sowerby)
Bradford, Dewsbury, Huddersfield, Keighley, Rochdale, Saddleworth, Todmorden

HALSTEAD, ESS. (Hedingham)
Braintree, Lexden, Risbridge, Sudbury, Witham

HALTWHISTLE, NBL.
Alston, Bellingham, Brampton, Hexham. Penrith

HAMBLEDON, SRY. (Cranley, Witley)
Dorking, Farnham, Guildford, Midhurst, Petworth

HAMPSTEAD, LND.
Barnet, Edmonton, Hendon, Kensington, Marylebone, Pancras

HARDINGSTONE, NTH. (Brafield, Milton)
Newport Pagnell, Northampton, Potterspury, Towester, Wellingborough

HARTISMERE, SFK. (Botesdale, Eye, Mendlesham)
Bosmere, Depwade, Guiltcross, Hoxne, Plumesgate, Stour

HARTLEPOOL, DUR.
Durham, Easington, Stockton

HARTLEY WINTNEY, HAM. (Farnborough, Odiham)
Alton, Basingstoke, Easthampstead, Farnborough, Farnham, Wokingham

HASLINGDEN, LAN. (Accrington, Edenfield, Newchurch, Rossendale)
Blackburn, Bolton, Burnley, Bury, Clitheroe, Rochdale, Todmorden

HASTINGS, SSX. (Ore)
Battle, Rye

HATFIELD, HRT. (Welwyn)
Barnet, Edmonton, Hertford, Hitchin, St Albans

HAVANT, HAM.
Catherington, Fareham, Portsea Island, Westbourne, Westhampnett

HAVERFORDWEST, PEM. (Fishguard, Milford, St Davids)
Cardigan, Narberth, Pembroke

HAY, BRE. (Clyro, Talgarth)
Brecknock, Builth, Crickhowell, Hereford, Presteigne, Weobley

HAYFIELD, DBY. (Glossop)
Ashton-under-Lyne, Chapel-en-le-Frith, Huddersfield, Macclesfield, Saddleworth, Stockport

HEADINGTON, OXF. (St Clements, Wheatley)
Abingdon, Bicester, Oxford, Thame, Woodstock

HELMSLEY, YKS. (Kirkby Moorside, Oswaldkirk)
Easingwold, Guisborough, Malton, Northallerton, Pickering, Stokesley, Thirsk

HELSTON, CON. (Breage, Crowan, St Keverne, Wendron)
Falmouth, Redruth, Truro

HEMEL HEMPSTEAD, HRT. (Flamstead, Kings Langley)
Amersham, Berkhamstead, Leighton Buzzard, Luton, St Albans, Watford

HEMSWORTH, YKS.
Barnsley, Doncaster, Pontefract, Wakefield

HENDON, MDX. (Edgware, Harrow, Willesden)
Barnet, Brentford, Hammersmith, Hampstead, Kensington, Marylebone, Uxbridge Watford

HENLEY, OXF. (Watlington)
Abingdon, Bradfield, Reading, Thame, Wallingford, Wokingham, Wycombe

HENSTEAD, NFK. (Humbleyard)
Blofield, Depwade, Forehoe, Loddon, Norwich, St Faiths

HEREFORD, HEF. (Burghill, Clodock, Dewchurch, Fownhope, Kentchurch, Madley)
Abergavenny, Bromyard, Hay, Ledbury, Leominster, Monmouth, Ross, Weobley

HERTFORD, HRT (Watton)
Edmonton, Hatfield, Hitchin, Royston, Ware

HEXHAM, NBL. (Allendale, Bywell, Chollerton)
Bellingham, Brampton, Castle Ward, Durham, Gateshead, Haltwhistle, Longtown, Weardale

HIGHWORTH, WIL. (Swindon)
Cirencester, Cricklade, Faringdon, Hungerford, Marlborough

HINCKLEY, LEI. (Burbage, Earl Shilton)
Atherstone, Barrow-upon-Soar, Blaby, Foleshill, Lutterworth, Market Bosworth, Nuneaton

HITCHIN, HRT. (Baldock)
Ampthill, Biggleswade, Hatfield, Hertford, Luton, Royston, St Albans

HOLBEACH, LIN. (Gedney Hill, Long Sutton)
Boston, Bourne Peterborough, Sleaford, Wisbech

HOLBECK, YKS. - previously part of Hunslet

HOLBORN, LND.
Clerkenwell, St Giles, St Luke, Strand

HOLLINGBOURN, KEN. (Headcorn, Lenham)
Cranbrook, Faversham, Maidstone, Medway, Milton, West Ashford

HOLSWORTHY, DEV. (Black Torrington, Broadwoodwidger, Clawton, Milton Demerel)
Bideford, Okehampton, Tavistock, Torrington

HOLYWELL, FLN. (Flint, Mold, Whitford)
Great Boughton, Ruthin, St Asaph, Wrexham

HONITON, DEV. (Ottery St Mary)
Axminster, Chard, St Thomas, Taunton, Wellington

HOO, KEN.
Medway, North Aylesford, Sheppey

HORNCASTLE, LIN. (Tattershall, Tetford, Wragby)
Boston, Caistor, Lincoln, Louth, Spilsby

HORSHAM, SSX.
Cuckfield, East Grinstead, Hambledon, Petworth, Reigate, Thakeham

HOUGHTON-LE-SPRING, DUR. (Hetton-le-Hole)
Chester-le-Street, Durham, Easington, Sunderland

HOWDEN, YKS. (Bubwith, Holme, Newport)
Beverley, Goole, Pocklington, Selby, York

HOXNE, SFK. (Dennington, Stradbroke)
Blything, Bosmere, Depwade, Hartismere, Plomesgate, Wangford

HUDDERSFIELD, YKS. (Almondbury, Golcar, Holmfirth, Honley, Kirkburton, Kirkheaton, Lockwood, Meltham, Newmill, Slaithwaite)
Bradford, Dewsbury, Halifax, Oldham, Rochdale, Saddleworth, Wakefield, Wortley

HULL, YKS. (Humber, Myton, St Mary)
Sculcoates

HUNGERFORD, BRK. (Kintbury, Lambourn)
Andover, Faringdon, Highworth, Kingsclere, Marlborough, Newbury, Pewsey, Wantage

HUNSLET, YKS. (Chapeltown, Holbeck, Kirkstall, Rothwell, Whitkirk, Wortley)
Bradford, Dewsbury, Leeds, Pontefract, Wakefield

HUNTINGDON, HUN. (Ramsey, Sawtry, Spaldwick)
Caxton, North Witchford, Oundle, Peterborough, St Ives, St Neots, Whittlesey

IPSWICH, SFK.
Bosmere, Samford, Woodbridge

ISLE OF WIGHT (Calbourne, Cowes, Godshill, Newport, Ryde)
Alverstoke, Fareham, Havant, Lymington, New Forest, Portsea Island

ISLINGTON, LND.
Clerkenwell, Edmonton, Hackney, Pancras, St Luke

KEIGHLEY, YKS. (Bingley, Haworth)
Bradford, Burnley, Halifax, Otley, Skipton, Todmorton

KENDAL, WES. (Ambleside, Grayrigg, Kirkby Lonsdale, Milnthorpe)
Bootle, Cockermouth, East Ward, Lancaster, Sedburgh, Ulverston, West Ward, Whitehaven

KENSINGTON, LND. (Brompton, Fulham, Hammersmith, Paddington)
Brentford, Chelsea, Hampstead, Hendon, Marylebone,St George Hanover Square

KETTERING, NTH. (Corby, Rothwell)
Brixworth, Market Harborough, Oundle, Thrapston, Uppingham, Wellingborough

KEYNSHAM, SOM. (Bitton, Newton, Oldland)
Bath, Bedminster, Bristol, Chipping Sodbury, Clifton, Clutton

KIDDERMINSTER, WOR. (Bewdley, Chaddesley-Corbett, Lower Mitton, Wolverley)
Bridgnorth, Bromsgrove, Cleobury Mortimer, Droitwich, Martley, Stourbridge, Wolverhampton

KINGSBRIDGE, DEV. (Blackawton, Modbury, Stokenham, West Alvington)
Plympton St Mary, Totnes

KINGSCLERE, HAM. (Highclere)
Andover, Basingstoke, Bradfield, Hungerford, Newbury, Whitchurch

KINGS LYNN, NFK.
Downham, Freebridge Lynn, Wisbech

KINGS NORTON, WOR. (Edgbaston, Harborne)
Alcester, Aston, Birmingham, Bromsgrove, Solihull, Stourbridge, Stratford-on-Avon, West Bromwich

KINGSTON, SRY. (Esher, Hampton, Wimbledon)
Brentford, Chertsey, Croydon, Epsom, Richmond, Wandsworth

KINGTON, HEF. (Brilley, Kinsham, Radnor) - previously part of Knighton and Presteigne

KIRK DEIGHTON, YKS. - later part of Wetherby
Great Ouseburn, Knaresborough, Tadcaster, Wetherby, York

KNARESBOROUGH, YKS. (Harogate)
Great Ouseburn, Kirk Deighton, Otley, Pateley Bridge, Wetherby

KNIGHTON, RAD. (Llanbister)
Builth, Ludlow, Newtown, Presteigne, Rhayader

LAMBETH, LND. (Brixton, Kennington, Norwood, Waterloo)
Camberwell, Newington, St George Southwark, St Olave, St Saviour, Wandsworth

LAMPETER, CGN. (Llanbyther, Llandyssil, Penbryn)
Aberayon, Llandilofawr, Llandovery, Newcastle-in-Emlyn, Tregdron

LANCASTER, LAN. (Arkholme, Caton, Ellel, Heaton, Tunstal, Wharton, Wray)
Clitheroe, Garstang, Kendal, Settle

LANCHESTER, DUR. (Tanfield) - previously part of Durham

LANGPORT, SOM. (Curry-Rivell, Somerton)
Bridgwater, Chard, Taunton, Wells, Wincanton, Yeovil

LAUNCESTON, CON. (Alternon, Northill, North Petherwin, St Stephens,

LEDBURY, HER. (Yarkhill)
Bromyard, Hereford, Martley, Newent, Ross, Upton-upon-Severn

LEEDS, YKS. (Chapeltown, Kirkstall)
Bradford, Hunslet, Pontefract, Rothwell, Tadcaster, Wharfedale

LEEK, STS. (Longnot, Norton)
Ashborne, Bakewell, Cheadle, Congleton, Macclesfield, Stoke-upon-Trent, Wolstanton

LEICESTER, LEI.
Barrow-upon-Soar, Billesdon, Blaby, Market Bosworth

LEIGH, LAN. (Atherton, Culcheth, Lowton, Westleigh)
Bolton, Salford, Warrington, Wigan

LEIGHTON BUZZARD, BDF. (Eddlesborough, Ivinghoe, Wing)
Aylesbury, Berhamstead, Hemel Hempstead, Luton, Newport Pagnell, Winslow, Woburn

LEOMINSTER, HEF. (Bodenham, Kingsland)
Bromyard, Hereford, Ludlow, Presteigne, Tenbury, Weobley

LEWES, SSX. (Chailey, Ditchling, Newhaven, Rottingdean, Westfirle)
Brighton, Cuckfield, Eastbourne, East Grinstead, Hailsham, Steyning, Uckfield

LEWISHAM, LND. (Eltham, Lee, Plumstead, Sydenham)
Battersea, Bromley, Camberwell, Greenwich

LEXDEN, ESS. (Dedham, Fordham, Peldon, Stanway, Wivenhoe)
Colchester, Halstead, Maldon, Samford, Sudbury, Tendring, Witham

LEYBURN, YKS. (Middleham)
Askrigg, Bedale, Reeth, Richmond, Ripon, Settle, Skipton

LICHFIELD, STS. (Rugeley, Yoxall)
Burton, Penkridge, Stafford, Tamworth, Uttoxeter, Walsall

LINCOLN, LIN.
Caistor, Gainsborough, Horncastle, Newark, Sleaford

LINTON, CAM. (Balsham, Duxford)
Chesterton, Newmarket, Risbridge, Royston, Saffron Walden

LISKEARD, CON. (Callington, Lerrin, Looe)
Bodmin, Camelford, Launceston, St Austell, St Germans, Tavistock

LIVERPOOL, LAN.
Birkenhead, Prescot, West Derby

LLANDILOFAWR, CMN. (Llandebie, Llandilo, Llanfynydd, Llangathen, Talley)
Carmarthen, Lampeter, Llandovery, Llanelly, Neath, Newcastle-in-Emlyn

LLANDOVERY, CMN. (Cilycwm, Conwil-Gayo, Llanddausaint, Llandingat, Llanfairarybryn, Llangadock, Llansadwen, Llanwrtyd, Myddfai)
Brecknock, Builth, Carmarthon, Llandilofawr, Neath, Tregaron

LLANELLY, CMN. (Llannon, Loughor, Pembrey)
Carmarthon, Gower, Llandilofawr, Neath, Swansea

LLANFYLLIN, MGY. (Llanfair, Llansaintffraid, Llanrhaiadr)
Atcham, Bala, Corwen, Dolgelly, Machynlleth, Montgomery, Newtown, Oswestry

LLANRWST, DEN. (Bettws-y-Coed, Yspytty)
Bala, Bangor, Carnarvon, Conway, Corwen, Festiniog, St Asaph

LODDON, NFK. (Aldeby, Woodton)
Blofield, Depwade, Henstead, Mutford, Wangford

LONDON CITY, LND.
Clerkenwell, East Ham, St George-in-the-East, Strand, Whitechapel

LONGTOWN, CUL. (High Longtown, Low Longtown)
Bellingham, Brampton, Carlisle

LOUGHBOROUGH, LEI. (Leake)
Ashby-de-la-Zouch, Barrow-upon-Soar, Basford, Bingham, Market Bosworth, Melton Mowbray, Shardlow

LOUTH, LIN. (Binbrook, Saltfleet, Tetney, Wilhern)
Caistor, Horncastle, Spilsby

LUDLOW, SAL. (Cainham, Diddlesbury, Leintwardine, Munslow)
Bridgnorth, Church Stretton, Cleobury Mortimer, Clun, Knighton, Leominster, Presteigne, Tenbury

LUNESDALE, LAN. (Arkholme, Caton, Tunstal, Wray) - previously part of Lancaster

LUTON, BDF. (Dunstable)
Ampthill, Hemel Hempstead, Hitchin, Leighton Buzzard, St Albans, Woburn

LUTTERWORTH, LEI.
Blaby, Brixworth, Foleshill, Hinckley, Market Harborough, Rugby

LYMINGTON, HAM. (Milford)
Christchurch, Isle of Wight, New Forest

MACCLESFIELD, CHS. (Alderley, Bollington, Gawsworth, Prestbury, Rainow, Sutton)
Altrincham, Bakewell, Chapel-en-le-Frith, Congleton, Hayfield, Leek, Northwich, Stockport

MACHYNLLETH, MGY. (Darowen, Pennel)
Aberystwyth, Dolgelly, Llanfyllin, Newtown

MADELEY, SAL. (Broseley, Dawley, Much Wenlock)
Atcham, Bridgnorth, Church Stretton, Shifnal, Wellington

MAIDSTONE, KEN. (Loose, Marden, Yalding)
Cranbrook, Hollingbourn, Malling, Tunbridge

MALDON, ESS. (Bradwell, Southminster, Tollesbury)
Chelmsford, Lexden, Rochford, Witham

MALLING, KEN. (Aylesford, East Peckham, Wrotham)
Dartford, Hollingbourn, Maidstone, Medway, North Aylesford, Sevenoaks, Tunbridge

MALMESBURY, WIL.
Calne, Chippenham, Chipping Sodbury, Cirencester, Cricklade, Tetbury

MALTON, YKS. (Bulmer, Hovingham, Rillington, Westow)
Driffield, Easingwold, Helmsley, Pickering, Pocklington, Scarborough, York

MANCHESTER, LAN. (Ancoats, Blackley, Cheetham, Deansgate, Failsworth, London Road, Market Street, Newton, Prestwich, St George)
Ashton-under-Lyne, Barton-upon-Irwell, Bolton, Bury, Chorlton, Oldham, Salford

MANSFIELD, NTT. (Blackwell, Blidworth, Pleasley, Sutton-in-Ashfield, Warsop)
Basford, Belper, Chesterfield, Southwell, Worksop

MARKET BOSWORTH, LEI. (Ibstock)
Ashby-de-la-Zouch, Barrow-upon-Soar, Blaby, Hinckley, Loughborough, Tamworth

MARKET DRAYTON, SAL. (Hodney, Moreton Say)
Nantwich, Newcastle-under-Lyme, Newport, Stone, Wellington, Wem, Whitchurch

MARKET HARBOROUGH, LEI.
Billesdon, Blaby, Brixworth, Kettering, Lutterworth, Uppingham

MARLBOROUGH, WIL.
Calne, Cricklade, Devizes, Highworth, Hungerford, Pewsey

MARTLEY, WOR. (Holt, Leigh, Witley)
Bromyard, Cleobury Minster, Droitwich, Kidderminster, Tenbury, Upton-upon-Severn, Worcester

MARYLEBONE, LND.
Hampstead, Kensington, Pancras, St Giles, St James Westminster

MEDWAY, KEN. (Gillingham, Rochester)
Hollingbourn, Hoo, Malling, Milton, North Aylesford

MELKSHAM, WIL. (Trowbridge)
Bradford-on-Avon, Calne, Chippenham, Devizes, Westbury

MELTON MOWBRAY, LEI. (Clawson, Somerby, Waltham)
Barrow-upon-Soar, Billesdon, Bingham, Grantham, Loughborough, Oakham

MERE, WIL.
Frome, Shaftesbury, Tisbury, Warminster, Wincanton

MERIDEN, WAR. (Coleshill)
Aston, Coventry, Foleshill, Nuneaton, Solihull, Warwick

MERTHYR TYDFIL, GLA. (Aberdare, Gelligaer)
Bedwellty, Brecknock, Bridgend, Cardiff, Crickhowell, Neath, Newport

MIDDLESBROUGH, YKS. (Ormesby, Thornaby) - previously part of Stockton and Stokesley

MIDHURST, SSX. (Fernhurst, Harting)
Chichester, Farnham, Hambledon, Petersfield, Westbourne

MILDENHALL, SFK. (Lakenheath, Worlington)
Ely, Newmarket, Thetford, Thingoe

MILE END OLD TOWN, LND.
Bethnal Green, Poplar, Stepney, West Ham, Whitechapel

MILTON, KEN.
Faversham, Hollingbourn, Hoo, Medway, Sheppey

MITFORD, NFK. (Bawdeswell, East Dereham, Liteham, Mattishall, North Elmham, Shipdham)
Aylsham, Forehoe, Freebridge Lynn, Swaffham, St Faiths, Wayland, Walsingham

MONMOUTH, MON. (Coleford, Dingestow, Trelleck)
Abergavenny, Chepstow, Hereford, Ross, Westbury-on-Severn

MONTGOMERY, MGY. (Chirlbury, Pool, Welshpool)
Atcham, Clun, Llanfyllin, Newtown

MORPETH, NBL. (Bedlington)
Alnwick, Bellingham, Castle Ward, Rothbury, Tynemouth

MUTFORD, SFK. (Gorleston, Kessingland, Lowestoft)
Blofield, Blything, Flegg, Loddon, Wangford, Yarmouth

NANTWICH, CHS. (Bunbury, Wrenbury, Wybunbury)
Congleton, Ellesmere, Great Boughton, Northwich, Market Drayton, Whitchurch, Wolstanton, Wrexham

NARBERTH, PEM. (Amroth, Begelly, Llanboidy, Llandissilio)
Cardigan, Carmarthon, Haverfordwest, Pembroke

NEATH, GLA. (Cadoxton, Llansamlet, Margam, Ystradgunlais, Ystradvelltry)
Brecknock, Bridgend, Cardiff, Llandilofawr, Llandovery, Llanelly, Merthyr Tydfil, Swansea

NEWARK, NTT. (Bassingham, Bennington, Claypole, North Collingham)
Bingham, East Retford, Grantham, Lincoln, Sleaford, Southwell

NEWBURY, BRK. (Speen, Thatcham)
Bradfield, Hungerford, Kingsclere, Wantage

NEWCASTLE-IN-EMLYN, CGN. (Kenarth, Llandyssil, Penbryn)
Aberayon, Cardigan, Carmarthon, Lampeter, Llandilofawr

NEWCASTLE-UNDER-LYME, STS. (Audley, Whitmore)
Market Drayton, Nantwich, Stoke-upon-Trent, Stone, Wolstanton

NEWCASTLE-UPON-TYNE, NBL. (Byker, Westgate)
Castle Ward, Gateshead, South Shields, Tynemouth

NEWENT, GLS. (Redmarley)
Gloucester, Ledbury, Ross, Tewkesbury, Upton-upon-Severn, Westbury-on-Severn

NEW FOREST, HAM. (Eling, Fawley, Lyndhurst)
Alderbury, Christchurch, Fordingbridge, Isle of Wight, Lymington, Ringwood, Romsey, Southampton, South Stoneham

NEWINGTON, LND.
Bermondsey, Camberwell, St George Southwark, St Olave, St Saviour

NEWMARKET, CAM. (Bottisham, Cheveley, Gazeley, Soham)
Chesterton, Ely, Linton, Mildenhall, Risbridge

NEWPORT, MON. (Caerleon, Mynyddyslwyn, St Woollos)
Bedwellty, Cardiff, Chepstow, Merthyr Tydfil, Pontypool

NEWPORT, SAL. (Gnosall)
Market Drayton, Penkridge, Shifnal, Stafford, Stone, Wellington

NEWPORT PAGNELL, BKM. (Fenny Stratford, Olney)
Ampthill, Bedford, Buckingham, Hardingstone, Leighton Buzzard,
Potterspury, Wellingborough, Winslow, Woburn

NEWTON ABBOT, DEV. (Ashburton, Chudleigh, Hampstead, Moreton,
Teignmouth, Torbay)
Crediton, Okehampton, St Thomas, Tavistock, Totnes

NEWTOWN, MGY. (Kerry, Llanidloes, Llanwnog, Tregynon)
Aberystwyth, Clun, Knighton, Llanfyllion, Machynlleth, Montgomery,
Rhayader

NORTHALLERTON, YKS. (Appleton-upon-Wiske)
Bedale, Darlington, Helmsley, Richmond, Stockton, Stokesley, Thirsk

NORTHAMPTON, NTH. (Bugbrooke)
Brixworth, Daventry, Hardingstone, Towcester, Wellingborough

NORTH AYLESFORD, KEN. (Northfleet, Strood)
Dartford, Gravesend, Hoo, Malling, Medway

NORTHLEACH, GLS. (Bibery, Chedworth)
Cheltenham, Cirencester, Faringdon, Stow-on-the-Wold, Winchcomb, Witney

NORTHWICH, CHS. (Middlewich, Over, Weaverham)
Altrincham, Congleton, Great Boughton, Macclesfield, Nantwich, Runcorn

NORTH WITCHFORD, CAM. (Chatteris, March)
Ely, Huntingdon, St Ives, Whittlesey, Wisbech

NORWICH, NFK. (Coslany, Conisford, East Wymer, Mancroft, West Wymer)
Blofield, Forehoe, Henstead, St Faiths

NOTTINGHAM, NTT. (Byron Castle, Exchange, Park, Sherwood)
Basford, Bingham, Radford

NUNEATON, WAR.
Atherstone, Coventry, Foleshill, Hinckley, Meriden

OAKHAM, RUT.
Billesdon, Bourne, Grantham, Melton Mowbray, Oundle, Stamford,
Uppingham

OKEHAMPTON, DEV. (Bratton Clovelly, Chagford, Hatherleigh, North
Tawton)
Crediton, Holsworthy, Newton Abbot, Tavistock, Torrington

OLDHAM, LAN. (Chadderton, Crompton, Middleton, Royton)
Ashton-under-Lyne, Bury, Manchester, Rochdale, Saddleworth

ONGAR, ESS. (Bobbingworth, Chipping Ongar)
Billericay, Chelmsford, Dunmow, Epping, Romford

ORMSKIRK, LAN. (Aughton, Bickerstaffe, Formby, Halsall, Lathom, North Meols, Scarisbrooke, Tarleton)
Chorley, Prescot, Preston, West Derby, Wigan

ORSETT, ESS. (Grays)
Billericay, Romford

OSWESTRY, SAL. (Knockin, Llansilin)
Atcham, Corwen, Ellesmere, Llanfyllin

OTLEY, YKS. (Harewood) - later part of Wharfedale
Bradford, Keighley, Knaresborough, Pateley Bridge, Skipton, Wetherby, Wharfedale

OUNDLE, NTH. (Fotheringhay, Weldon)
Huntingdon, Kettering, Peterborough, Stamford, Thrapston, Uppingham

OXFORD, OXF.
Abingdon, Headington, Woodstock

PANCRAS, LND. (Camden Town, Kentish Town)
Barnet, Clerkenwell, Edmonton, Hampstead, Holborn, Islington, Marylebone, St Giles

PATELEY BRIDGE, YKS. (Dacre Banks, Ramsgill, Thornthwaite)
Knaresborough, Otley, Ripon, Skipton, Wetherby

PATRINGTON, YKS.
Hull, Sculcoates, Skirlaugh

PEMBROKE, PEM. (Roose, Tenby)
Haverfordwest, Narberth

PENKRIDGE, STS. (Brewood, Cannock)
Lichfield, Newport, Shifnal, Stafford, Walsall, Wolverhampton

PENRITH, CUL. (Greystoke, Kirkoswald)
Alston, Brampton, Carlisle, Cockermouth, East Ward, Haltwhistle, West Ward, Wigton

PENZANCE, CON. (Marazion, St Buryan, St Ives, St Just-in-Penwith, Uny Lelant)
Helston, Redruth, Scilly Islands

PERSHORE, WOR. (Eckington, Upton Snodsbury)
Alcester, Droitwich, Evesham, Tewkesbury, Upton-upon-Severn, Worcester

PETERBOROUGH, NTH. (Crowland, Stilton, Thorney)
Bourne, Holbeach, Huntingdon, Oundle, Stamford, Whittlesey, Wisbech

PETERSFIELD, HAM. (East Meon)
Alresford, Alton, Catherington, Droxford, Midhurst, Westbourne

PETWORTH, SSX. (Billinghurst)
Chichester, Dorking, Hambledon, Horsham, Midhurst, Thakeham

PEWSEY, WIL. (Collingbourne, Netheravon)
Amesbury, Andover, Devizes, Hungerford, Marlborough

PICKERING, YKS. (Allerston, Lastingham, Lockton, Sinnington)
Guisborough, Helmsley, Malton, Scarborough, Stokesley, Whitby

PLOMESGATE, SFK. (Aldeborough, Earl Soham, Framlingham, Orford, Saxmundham, Wickham Market)
Blything, Bosmere, Hoxne, Woodbridge

PLYMOUTH, DEV.
East Stonehouse, Plympton St Mary, Stoke Damerel

PLYMPTON ST MARY, DEV. (Yealmpton)
East Stonehouse, Kingsbridge, Plymouth, Stoke Damerel, Tavistock, Totnes

POCKLINGTON, YKS. (East Stamford Bridge, Market Weighton)
Beverley, Driffield, Howden, Malton, York

PONTARDAWE, GLA. - previously part of Neath

PONTEFRACT, YKS. (Castleford, Kippax, Knottingley, Whitley)
Doncaster, Goole, Hemsworth, Hunslet, Selby, Tadcaster, Wakefield

PONTYPOOL, MON. (Llangibby, Usk)
Abergavenny, Bedwellty, Chepstow, Monmouth, Newport

PONTYPRIDD, GLA. (Llantrisaint, Ystradyfodwg) - previously part of Cardiff and Merthyr Tydfil

POOLE, DOR. (Canford, Lytchett)
Christchurch, Wareham, Wimborne

POPLAR, LND. (Bow)
Mile End Old Town, St George in the East, Stepney, West Ham, Whitechapel

PORTSEA ISLAND, HAM. (Kingston, Landport, Portsmouth Town)
Alverstoke, Fareham, Havant, Isle of Wight

POTTERSPURY, NTH.
Buckingham, Hardingstone, Newport Pagnell, Towester, Winslow

PRESCOT, LAN. (Farnworth, Hale, Huyton, Much Woolton, Rainford, St Helens)
Liverpool, Ormskirk, Warrington, West Derby, Wigan

PRESTON, LAN. (Alston, Broughton, Longton, Walton-le-Dale)
Blackburn, Chorley, Clitheroe, Fylde, Garstang, Lancaster, Ormskirk

PRESTEIGNE, RAD. (Beilley, Kington, Radnor)
Builth, Hay, Knighton, Leominster, Ludlow, Rhayader, Weobley

PWLLHELI, CAE. (Aberdaron, Criccieth, Nevin)
Carnarvon, Festiniog

RADFORD, NTT. (Hyson Green, Lenton, Snenton)
Basford, Bingham, Nottingham

READING, BRK.
Bradfield, Henley, Wokingham

REDRUTH, CON. (Camborne, Gwennap, Illogan, Phillack)
Falmouth, Helsdon, Penzance, Truro

REETH, YKS. (Muker)
Askrigg, East Ward, Leyburn, Richmond, Teesdale

REIGATE, SRY. (Horley)
Croydon, Dorking, East Grinstead, Epsom, Godstone, Horsham

RHAYADER, RAD. (Nantmel)
Aberystwyth, Builth, Knighton, Newtown, Presteigne, Tregaron

RICHMOND, SRY. (Mortlake)
Brentford, Kensington, Kingston, Wandsworth

RICHMOND, YKS. (Aldbrough, Catterick, Newsham)
Askrigg, Bedale, Darlington, Leyburn, Northallerton, Reeth, Teesdale

RINGWOOD, HAM.
Christchurch, Fordingbridge, New Forest, Wimborne

RIPON, YKS. (Dishforth, Kirkby Malzeard, Wath)
Bedale, Easingwold, Great Ouseburn, Knaresborough, Leyburn, Pateley Bridge, Skipton, Thirsk

RISBRIDGE, SFK. (Clare, Haverhill, Wickhambrook)
Braintree, Dunmow, Halstead, Newmarket, Saffron Walden, Sudbury, Thingoe

ROCHDALE, LAN. (Blatchinworth, Butterworth, Castleton, Spotland, Wardleworth, Whitworth, Wuerdle)
Burnley, Bury, Halifax, Haslingden, Huddersfield, Oldham, Saddleworth, Todmorden

ROCHFORD, ESS. (Great Wakering, Prittleswell, Rayleigh)
Billericay, Chelmsford, Maldon

ROMFORD, ESS. (Barking, Hornchurch, Ilford)
Billericay, Epping, Ongar, Orsett, West Ham

ROMNEY MARSH, KEN. (Lydd, New Romney)
East Ashford, Elham

ROMSEY, HAM. (Michelmersh)
Alderbury, New Forest, South Stoneham, Stockbridge, Winchester

ROSS, HEF. (St Weonards, Sollershope)
Hereford, Ledbury, Monmouth, Newent, Westbury-on-Severn

ROTHBURY, NBL. (Elsdon)
Alnwick, Bellingham, Glendale, Morpeth

ROTHERHAM, YKS. (Beighton, Kimberley, Maltby, Wath)
Doncaster, Ecclesfield Bierlow, Hemsworth, Sheffield, Worksop, Wortley

ROTHERHITHE, LND.
Bermondsey, Camberwell, Greenwich

ROYSTON,HRT. (Buntingford, Melbourn)
Biggleswade, Bishop Stortford, Caxton, Chesterton, Hertford, Hitchin, Luton, Ware

RUGBY, WAR. (Crick, Dunchurch)
Brixworth, Coventry, Daventry, Foleshill, Lutterworth, Southam, Warwick

RUNCORN, CHS. (Budworth, Daresbury, Frodsham)
Altrincham, Great Boughton, Northwich, Warrington

RUTHIN, DEN. (Gyffylliog, Llanarmon, Llandyrnog, Llanelidan, Llanrhaiadr)
Corwen, Holywell, Llanrwst, St Asaph, Wrexham

RYE, SSX. (Beckley)
Battle, Cranbrook, East Ashford, Hastings, Romney Marsh, Tenterden, Ticehurst

SADDLEWORTH, YKS. (Delph, Upper Mill)
Ashton-under-Lyne, Halifax, Huddersfield, Oldham, Rochdale

SAFFRON WALDEN, ESS. (Newport, Radwinter)
Bishop Stortford, Braintree, Dunmow, Linton, Royston, Risbridge

ST ALBANS, HRT. (Harpenden)
Barnet, Hatfield, Hitchin, Hemel Hempstead, Leighton Buzzard, Luton, Watford

ST ASAPH, DEN. (Abergele, Denbigh)
Conway, Holywell, Ruthin, Llanrwst

ST AUSTELL, CON. (Fowey, Grampound, Mevagissey)
Bodmin, Liskeard, St Columb, Truro

ST COLUMB, CON. (Newlyn, Padstow)
Bodmin, St Austell, Truro

ST FAITHS, NFK. (Sprowston)
Aylsham, Blofield, Forehoe, Henstead, Mitford, Norwich, Tunstead

ST GEORGE HANOVER SQUARE, LND. (Belgrave, Mayfair)
Chelsea, Kensington, St Giles, St James Westminster

ST GEORGE IN THE EAST, LND.
London City, Stepney, West Ham

ST GEORGE SOUTHWARK, LND.
Bermondsey, Lambeth, Newington

ST GERMANS, CON. (Antony, Saltash)
Liskeard, Plympton, Tavistock

ST GILES, LND.
Holborn, Marylebone, Pancras, St George Hanover Square, St Martin-in-the-Fields, Shoreditch, Strand

ST IVES, HUN. (Somersham, Swavesley, Warboys)
Caxton, Chesterton, Haddenham, Huntingdon, North Witchford, St Neots

ST JAMES WESTMINSTER, LND.
Kensington, St George Hanover Square, St Giles, St Martin-in-the-Fields, Westminster

ST LUKE, LND. (City Road, Finsbury, Old Street, Whitecross Street)
Clerkenwell, Holborn, Islington

ST MARTIN-IN-THE-FIELDS, LND. (Charing Cross, Long Acre)
Holborn, St George Hanover Square, St Giles, St James Westminster, Strand, Westminster

ST NEOTS, HUN. (Kimbolton)
Biggleswade, Caxton, Huntingdon, St Ives, Thrapston

ST OLAVE SOUTHWARK, LND.
Bermondsey, Lambeth, Newington, St Saviour Southwark

ST SAVIOUR SOUTHWARK, LND.
Bermondsey, Lambeth, Newington, St Olave Southwark

ST THOMAS, DEV. (Alphington, Broad Clist, Christow, East Budleigh, Exmouth, Heavitree, Kenton, Topsham, Woodbury)
Crediton, Exeter, Honiton, Newton Abbot, Okehampton, Tiverton

SALFORD, LAN. (Broughton, Greengate, Pendleton, Regent Road)
Barton-upon-Irwell, Bolton, Chorlton, Leigh, Manchester, Warrington

SALISBURY, WIL.
Alderbury, Fordingbridge, Wilton

SAMFORD, SFK. (Capel St Mary, Holbrook)
Bosmere, Cosford, Ipswich, Lexden, Sudbury, Tendring, Woodbridge

SCARBOROUGH, YKS. (Filey, Hutton-Bushell, Sherburn)
Bridlington, Driffield, Malton, Pickering, Whitby

SCILLY ISLES
Penzance

SCULCOATES, YKS. (Cottingham, Drypool, Ferryby, Hedon, Hessle, Sutton)
Beverley, Hull, Patrington, Skirlaugh

SEDBURGH, YKS. (Dent, Garsdale)
Askrigg, East Ward, Kendal, Settle

SELBY, YKS. (Carlton, Riccall)
Goole, Howden, Pontefract, Tadcaster, York

SETTLE, YKS. (Arncliffe, Bentham, Kirkby, Long Preston, Malham)
Askrigg, Clitheroe, Lancaster, Leyburn, Skipton

SEVENOAKS, KEN. (Penshurst, Shoreham)
Bromley, Dartford, Malling, East Grinstead, Godstone, Tunbridge

SHARDLOW, DBY. (Castle Donington, Melbourne, Spondon, Stapleford)
Ashby-de-la-Zouch, Basford, Belper, Burton-upon-Trent, Loughborough

SHAFTESBURY DOR. (Fontmell, Gillingham)
Blandford, Mere, Sturminster, Tisbury, Wimborne, Wincanton

SHEFFIELD, YKS. (Attercliffe, Brightside, Handsworth)
Chesterfield, Ecclesall Bierlow, Rotherham, Wortley

SHEPPEY, KEN. (Eastchurch, Minster in Sheppey)
Faversham, Hoo, Milton

SHEPTON MALLET, SOM. (Evercreech, Stoke Lane)
Bath, Clutton, Frome, Wells, Wincanton

SHERBORNE, DOR. (Bradford Abbas, Yetminster)
Beaminster, Dorchester, Sturminster, Wincanton, Yeovil

SHIFNAL, SAL. (Albrighton)
Bridgnorth, Madeley, Newport, Penkridge, Stafford, Wellington, Wolverhampton

SHIPSTON-ON-STOUR, WAR. (Halford, Moreton, Stour Campden)
Banbury, Chipping Norton, Evesham, Southam, Stow-on-the-Wold,Stratford-on-Avon, Winchcomb

SHOREDITCH, LND. (Haggerston, Holywell, Hoxton, St Leonard)
Bethnal Green, Hackney, St Giles, West Ham

SHREWSBURY, SAL.
Atcham

SKIPTON, YKS. (Addingham, Barnoldswick, Gargrave, Grassington, Kettlewell, Kildwick)
Burnley, Clitheroe, Keighley, Leyburn, Otley, Pateley Bridge, Settle

SKIRLAUGH, YKS. (Aldbrough, Brandesburton, Hornsea, Humbleton)
Beverley, Bridlington, Driffield, Patrington, Sculcoates

SLEAFORD, LIN. (Aswarby, Billinghay, Heckington, Leadenham)
Boston, Bourne, Grantham, Holbeach, Horncastle, Lincoln, Newark

SMALLBURGH, NFK. - previously known as Tunstead

SOLIHULL, WAR. (Knowle, Tanworth)
Birmingham, Kings Norton, Meriden, Stratford-on-Avon, Warwick

SOUTHAM, WAR.
Banbury, Daventry, Rugby, Shipston-on-Stour, Stratford-on-Avon, Warwick

SOUTHAMPTON, HAM.
New Forest Romsey, South Stoneham

SOUTH MOLTON, DEV. (Chulmleigh, Witheridge)
Barnstaple, Crediton, Dulverton, Okehampton, Torrington, Tiverton

SOUTH SHIELDS, DUR. (Westoe)
Chester-le-Street, Gateshead, Newcastle-upon-Tyne, Sunderland, Tynemouth

SOUTH STONEHAM, HAM. (Millbrook, St Mary Extra)
Droxford, Fareham, New Forest, Romsey, Southampton, Winchester

SOUTHWELL, NTT. (Kneesal)
Basford, Bingham, East Retford, Mansfield, Newark, Worksop

SPALDING, LIN. (Deeping St Nicholas, Donington, Gosberton, Moulton, Pinchbeck)
Boston, Bourne, Holbeach, Peterborough, Sleaford

SPILSBY, LIN. (Alford, Burgh, Stickney, Wainfleet)
Boston, Horncastle, Louth

STAFFORD, STS. (Castle Church, Colwich)
Lichfield, Newport, Penkridge, Stone, Uttoxeter

STAINES, MDX. (Sunbury)
Brentford, Chertsey, Eton, Kingston, Uxbridge, Windsor

STAMFORD, LIN. (Barnack)
Bourne, Oakham, Oundle, Peterborough, Uppingham

STEPNEY, LND. (Limehouse, Ratcliff, Shadwell)
Mile End Old Town, Poplar, St George-in-the-East, West Ham

STEYNING, SSX. (Shoreham)
Brighton, Cuckfield, Horsham, Lewes, Thakeham, Worthing

STOCKBRIDGE, HAM. (Broughton)
Andover, Alderbury, Amesbury, Romsey, Winchester

STOCKPORT, CHS. (Cheadle, Hazel Grove, Heaton Norris, Hyde, Marple)
Altrincham, Chorlton, Ashton-under-Lyne, Macclesfield

STOCKTON, DUR. (Sedgefield, Yarm)
Auckland, Darlington, Durham, Easington, Guisborough, Hartlepool, Northallerton, Stokesley

STOKE DAMEREL, DEV. (Clowance, Morice, St Aubyn, Stoke, Tamor)
East Stonehouse, Plymouth, Plympton St Mary

STOKE-UPON-TRENT, STS. (Fenton, Hanley, Longton, Shelton)
Cheadle, Leek, Newcastle-under-Lyme, Stone, Wolstanton

STOKESLEY, YKS. (Hutton)
Guisborough, Helmsley, Northallerton, Pickering, Stockton

STONE, STS. (Eccleshall, Trentham)
Cheadle, Market Drayton, Newcastle-under-Lyme, Newport, Stafford, Stoke-upon-Trent, Uttoxeter

STOURBRIDGE, WOR. (Halesowen, Kingswinford)
Bridgnorth, Bromsgrove, Dudley, Kidderminster, Kings Norton, West Bromwich, Wolverhampton

STOW, SFK. (Rattlesden, Stowmarket, Walsham-le-Willows)
Bosmere, Cosford, Guiltcross, Hartismere, Thetford, Thingoe

STOW-ON-THE-WOLD, GLS. (Bourton-on-the-Water)
Chipping Norton, Northleach, Shipston-on-Stour, Winchcomb, Witney

STRAND, LND.
Holborn, London City, St Giles, Westminster

STRATFORD-ON-AVON, WAR. (Kineton, Old Stratford, Wellesbourne, Wootton Wawen)
Alcester, Evesham, Shipston-on-Stour, Solihull, Southam, Warwick

STRATTON, CON. (Kilkhampton, Week St Mary)
Barnstaple, Camelford, Holsworthy, Launceston

STROUD, GLS. (Bisley, Horsley, Minchinhampton, Painswick, Rodborough, Stonehouse)
Cheltenham, Cirencester, Dursley, Gloucester, Tetbury, Wheatenhurst

STURMINSTER, DOR. (Stalbridge)
Blandford, Dorchester, Shaftesbury, Sherborne, Wincanton

SUDBURY, SFK. (Bulmer, Bures, Hartest, Melford)
Cosford, Halstead, Lexden, Risbridge, Samford

SUNDERLAND, DUR. (Monkwearmouth, North Bishopswearmouth, South Bishopswearmouth)
Chester-le-Street, Easington, Gateshead, Houghton-le-Spring,South Shields

SWAFFHAM, NFK. (Saham-Toney)
Downham, Forehoe Lynn, Mitford, Thetford, Wayland

SWANSEA, GLA. (Llandilotalybont, Llangatelach)
Gower, Llanelly, Neath

TADCASTER, YKS. (Aberford, Appleton Roebuck, Bitton, Bramham)
Great Ouseburn, Kirk Deighton, Pontefract, Selby, Wetherby, York

TAMWORTH, STS. (Fazeley)
Ashby-de-la-Zouch, Aston, Atherstone, Burton-upon-Trent, Lichfield, Market Bosworth, Meriden

TAUNTON, SOM. (Bishops Lydeard, North Curry, Pitminster)
Bridgwater, Chard, Honiton, Langport, Wellington, Williton

TAVISTOCK, DEV. (Buckland-Monachorum, Calstock, Lifton, Milton Abbot)
Holsworthy, Launceston, Newton Abbot, Okehampton, Plympton St Mary, St Germans, Totnes

TEESDALE, DUR. (Barnard Castle, Middleton, Staindrop)
Alston, Auckland, Darlington, East Ward, Reeth, Richmond, Weardale

TENBURY, WOR. (Bockleton)
Bromyard, Cleobury Mortimer, Leominster, Ludlow, Martley

TENDRING, ESS. (Ardley, Harwich, Manningtree, St Osyth, Thorpe)
Colchester, Lexden

TENTERDEN, KEN. (Rolvenden)
Cranbrook, Battle, East Ashford, Rye, Ticehurst, West Ashford

TETBURY, GLS. (Didmarton)
Chipping Sodbury, Cirencester, Dursley, Malmesbury, Stroud

TEWKESBURY, GLS. (Deerhurst, Overbury)
Cheltenham, Evesham, Gloucester, Newent, Pershore, Upton-upon-Severn, Winchcomb

THAKEHAM, SSX. (Pulborough, Washington)
Chichester, Horsham, Petworth, Steyning, Worthing

THAME, OXF. (Brill, Lewknor)
Abingdon, Aylesbury, Bicester, Headington, Henley, Wycombe

THANET, KEN. (Margate, Minster in Thanet, Ramsgate)
Blean, Eastry

THETFORD, NFK. (Methwold)
Downham, Ely, Guiltcross, Mildenhall, Stow, Swaffham, Thingoe, Wayland

THINGOE, SFK. (Fornham, Ixworth, Rougham)
Bury St Edmunds, Cosford, Mildenhall, Newmarket, Risbridge, Stow, Sudbury, Thetford

THIRSK, YKS. (Knayton, Pickhill, Sutton, Topcliffe)
Bedale, Easingwold, Helmsley, Northallerton, Ripon

THORNBURY, GLS. (Almondsbury, Berkeley)
Chepstow, Chipping Sodbury, Clifton, Dursley, Westbury-on-Severn, Wheatenhurst

THORNE, YKS. (Crowle, Epworth)
Doncaster, Gainsborough, Glanford Brigg, Goole

THRAPSTON, NTH. (Raunds)
Bedford, Kettering, Oundle, St Neots, Wellingborough

TICEHURST, SSX. (Frant, Salehurst, Wadhurst)
Battle, Cranbrook, East Grinstead, Hailsham, Rye, Tunbridge

TISBURY, WIL. (Donhead, Hindon)
Blandford Forum, Mere, Shaftesbury, Warminster, Wilton, Wimborne

TIVERTON, DEV. (Bampton, Cullampton, Silverton, Uffculme, Washfield)
Crediton, Dulverton, Honiton, St Thomas, South Molton, Wellington

TODMORDEN, YKS. (Hebden Bridge)
Burnley, Halifax, Haslingden, Keighley, Rochdale

TORRINGTON, DEV. (Dolton, High Bickington, Shebbear, Winkleigh)
Barnstaple, Bideford, Crediton, Holesworthy, Okehampton, South Molton

TOTNES, DEV. (Brixham, Buckfastleigh, Dartmouth, Harberton, Paignton, Ugborough)
Kingsbridge, Newton Abbot, Plympton St Mary, Tavistock

TOWCESTER, NTH. (Abthorpe)
Brackley, Buckingham, Daventry, Hardingstone, Northampton, Potterspury

TOXTETH PARK, LAN. - previously part of West Derby

TREGARON, CGN. (Gwynnws, Llangeitho)
Aberayon, Aberystwyth, Builth, Lampeter, Llandovery, Rhayader

TRURO, CON. (Kea, Kenwyn, Probus, St Agnes, St Clement, St Just)
Falmouth, Redruth, St Austell, St Columb

TUNBRIDGE, KEN. (Brenchley, Tunbridge Wells)
Cranbrook, East Grinstead, Maidstone, Malling, Sevenoaks, Ticehurst

TUNSTEAD, NFK. (Bacton, Ludham, Smallburgh, Stalham
Aylsham, Blofield, Erpingham, Flegg, St Faiths

TYNEMOUTH, NBL. (Blyth, Earsdon, Long Beaton, North Shields, Wallsend)
Castle Ward, Gateshead, Morpeth, Newcastle-upon-Tyne, South Shields

UCKFIELD, SSX. (Framfield, Isfield, Maresfield, Rotherfield)
Cuckfield, East Grinstead, Hailsham, Lewes, Ticehurst, Tunbridge

ULVERSTON, LAN. (Cartmel, Colton, Dalton, Hawkeshead, West Broughton)
Kendal, Bootle

UPPINGHAM, RUT. (Barrowden, Great Easton)
Billesdon, Kettering, Market Harborough, Oakham, Oundle, Stamford

UPTON-UPON-SEVERN, WOR. (Hanley, Kempsey)
Droitwich, Ledbury, Martley, Newent, Pershore, Tewkesbury, Worcester

UTTOXETER, STS. (Abbots Bromley, Sudbury)
Ashborne, Burton-upon-Trent, Cheadle, Lichfield, Stafford, Stone

UXBRIDGE, MDX. (Hayes, Hillingdon)
Brentford, Eton, Hendon, Staines, Watford

WAKEFIELD, YKS. (Alverthorpe, Ardsley, Bretton, Horbury, Oulton, Sandal, Stanley)
Barnsley, Dewsbury, Hemsworth, Huddersfield, Hunslet, Pontefract, Wortley

WALLINGFORD, BRK. (Cholsey)
Abingdon, Bradfield, Henley, Thame, Wantage

WALSALL, STS. (Aldridge, Bloxwich, Darlaston)
Aston, Dudley, Lichfield, Penkridge, West Bromwich, Wolverhampton

WALSINGHAM, NFK. (Fakenham, Wells)
Aylsham, Docking, Erpingham, Freebridge Lynn, Mitford

WANDSWORTH, LND. (Battersea, Clapham, Putney, Streatham)
Croydon, Lambeth, Kingston, Richmond

WANGFORD, SFK. (Beccles, Bungay)
Blything, Depwade, Hoxne, Loddon, Mutford

WANTAGE, BRK. (Hendred, Ilsley)
Abingdon, Bradfield, Faringdon, Hungerford, Newbury, Wallingford

WARE, HRT. (Hoddeston, Standon, Stanstead)
Bishop Stortford, Edmonton, Epping, Hatfield, Hertford, Royston

WAREHAM, DOR. (Bere Regis, Corfe Castle, Swanage)
Blandford, Dorchester, Poole, Weymouth, Wimborne

WARMINSTER, WIL. (Heytesbury, Longbridge-Deverill)
Amesbury, Devizes, Frome, Mere, Tisbury, Westbury, Wilton

WARRINGTON, LAN. (Letchford, Newton-in-Mackerfield, Rixton, Sankey, Winwick)
Altrincham, Leigh, Prescot, Runcorn, Wigan

WARWICK, WAR. (Budbrooke, Kenilworth, Leamington, Radford)
Coventry, Meriden, Rugby, Solihull, Southam, Stratford-on-Avon

WATFORD, HRT. (Abbots Langley, Bushey, Rickmansworth)
Amersham, Barnet, Eton, Hemel Hempstead, Hendon, St Albans, Uxbridge

WAYLAND, NFK. (Attleborough, Watton)
Depwade, Forehoe, Guiltcross, Mitford, Swaffham, Thetford

WEARDALE, DUR. (St John, Stanhope, Wolsingham)
Alston, Auckland, Durham, Hexham, Teesdale

WELLINGBOROUGH, NTH. (Earls Barton, Higham-Ferrers)
Bedford, Brixworth, Hardingstone, Kettering, Newport Pagnell, Northampton, St Neots, Thrapston

WELLINGTON, SAL. (Ercall Magna, Wombridge)
Atcham, Madeley, Market Drayton, Newport, Shifnal, Wem

WELLINGTON, SOM. (Culmstock, Milverton, Wiveliscombe)
Chard, Dulverton, Honiton, Taunton, Tiverton, Williton

WELLS, SOM. (Glastonbury)
Axbridge, Bridgwater, Clutton, Langport, Shepton Mallet, Wincanton

WEM, SAL. (Prees)
Atcham, Ellesmere, Market Drayton, Newport, Whitchurch

WEOBLEY, HEF. (Dilwyn)
Hay, Hereford, Leominster, Presteigne

WEST ASHFORD, KEN. (Calehill, Ashford)
Cranbrook, East Ashford, Faversham, Hollingbourn, Tenterden

WESTBOURNE, SSX. (Funtington)
Catherington, Chichester, Havant, Midhurst, Petersfield

WEST BROMWICH, STS. (Handsworth, Oldbury)
Aston, Birmingham, Dudley, Kings Norton, Walsall, Wolverhampton

WESTBURY, WIL. (Bradley, Edington)
Bradford-on-Avon, Devizes, Frome, Melksham, Warminster

WESTBURY-ON-SEVERN, GLS. (Huntley, Newnham)
Chepstow, Dursley, Gloucester, Monmouth, Ross, Thornbury, Wheatenhurst

WEST DERBY, LAN. (Crosby, Everton, Kirkdale, Litherland, Toxteth Park, Walton, Wavertree)
Liverpool, Ormskirk, Prescot

WEST HAM, ESS. (Leyton, Stratford, Walthamstow)
Bethnal Green, Edmonton, Epping, Hackney, Mile End Old Town, Poplar, Romford, Shoreditch, Stepney, St George in the East, Whitechapel

WESTHAMPNETT, SSX. (Boxgrove, Manhood, Singleton, Wyke, Yapton)
Chichester, Midhurst, Westbourne, Worthing

WEST LONDON, LND.
St George Hanover Square, Westminster

WESTMINSTER, LND.
Chelsea, St James Westminster, St Martin-in-the-Fields, Strand, West London

WEST WARD, WES. (Lowther, Morland)
Cockermouth, East Ward, Kendal, Penrith

WETHERBY, YKS. (Boston)
Kirk Deighton, Knaresborough, Otley, Pateley Bridge, Tadcaster

WEYMOUTH, DOR. (Abbotsbury, Portland, Upway)
Bridport, Dorchester, Wareham

WHARFEDALE, YKS. (Fewston, Horsforth, Yeadon)
Bradford, Leeds, Otley, Tadcaster, Wetherbv

WHEATENHURST, GLS. (Frampton, Haresfield)
Dursley, Gloucester, Stroud, Thornbury, Westbury-on-Severn

WHITBY, YKS. (Egton, Lythe)
Guisborough, Pickering, Scarborough

WHITCHURCH, HAM.
Andover, Basingstoke, Kingsclere, Winchester

WHITCHURCH, SAL. (Malpas)
Ellesmere, Market Drayton, Nantwich, Wem

WHITECHAPEL, LND. (Aldgate, Artillery, Spitalfields)
East London, London City, Mile End Old Town, Poplar, West Ham

WHITEHAVEN, CUL. (Egremont, Harrington, St Bees)
Bootle, Cockermouth, Kendal

WHITTLESEY, CAM.
Huntingdon, Peterborough, North Witchford, Wisbech

WIGAN, LAN. (Ashton-in-Mackerfield, Aspull, Hindley, Pemberton, Standish, Upholland)
Bolton, Chorley, Leigh, Ormskirk, Prescot, Warrington

WIGTON, CUL. (Abbey Hulme, Caldbeck)
Carlisle, Cockermouth, Penrith

WILLITON, SOM. (Dunster, Minehead, Stogumber, Stogursey)
Barnstaple, Bridgwater, Dulverton, Taunton, Wellington

WILTON, WIL. (Bishopstone)
Alderbury, Amesbury, Fordingbridge, Salisbury, Tisbury, Warminster, Wimborne

WIMBORNE, DOR. (Cranborne, Witchampton)
Blandford, Christchurch, Fordingbridge, Poole, Ringwood, Shaftesbury, Tisbury, Wareham, Wilton

WINCANTON, SOM. (Bruton, Castle Cary, Milborne Port)
Frome, Langport, Mere, Shepton Mallet, Sherborne, Wells, Yeovil

WINCHCOMB, GLS. (Cleeve, Guiting)
Cheltenham, Evesham, Northleach, Pershore, Shipston-on-Stour, Tewkesbury

WINCHESTER, HAM. (Hursley, Micheldever, The Worthys, Twyford)
Alresford, Alton, Andover, Basingstoke, Droxford, Romsey, South Stoneham, Stockbridge, Whitchurch

WINDSOR, BRK. (Egham)
Chertsey, Cookham, Easthampstead, Eton

WINSLOW, BKM.
Aylesbury, Buckingham, Leighton Buzzard, Newport Pagnell, Potterspury

WIRRAL, CHS. (Eastham, Neston, Woodchurch)
Birkenhead, Chester

WISBECH, CAM. (Leverington, Terrington St Clement, Upwell, Walpole St Peter, Walsoken)
Downham, Ely, Freebridge Lynn, Holbeach, Kings Lynn, North Witchford, Peterborough, Whittlesey

WITHAM, ESS. (Coggleshall, Kelvendon) - later part of Braintree

WITNEY, OXF. (Bampton, Burford, Ensham)
Abingdon, Chipping Norton, Faringdon, Northleach, Stow-on-the-Wold, Woodstock

WOBURN, BDF. (Toddington)
Ampthill. Leighton Buzzard, Luton, Newport Pagnell

WOKINGHAM, BRK. (Wargrave)
Basingstoke, Bradfield, Cookham, Easthampstead, Hartley Wintney, Henley, Reading

WOLSTANTON, STS. (Burslem, Tunstall)
Congleton, Leek, Newcastle-under-Lyme, Nantwich, Stoke-upon-Trent

WOLVERHAMPTON, STS. (Bilston, Kinfare, Tettenhall, Willenhall, Wombourn)
Bridgnorth, Dudley, Kidderminster, Penkridge, Shifnal, Stourbridge, Walsall, West Bromwich

WOODBRIDGE, SFK. (Carlford, Colness)
Bosmere, Ipswich, Plomesgate, Samford

WOODSTOCK, OXF. (Deddington)
Abingdon, Banbury, Bicester, Chipping Norton, Headington, Oxford, Witney

WOOLWICH, LND. (Plumstead) - Previously part of Greenwich

WORCESTER, WOR
Droitwich, Martley, Pershore, Upton-upon-Severn

WORKSOP, NTT. (Aston, Carburton, Carlton)
Doncaster, East Retford, Mansfield, Rotherham, Southwell

WORTHING, SSX. (Arundel, Broadwater, Littlehampton)
Brighton, Chichester, Thakeham, Westhampnett

WORTLEY, YKS. (Bradfield, Cawthorne, Ecclesfield, High Hoyland, Penistone)
Ashton-under-Lyne, Bakewell, Barnsley, Chapel-en-le-Frith, Ecclesall Bierlow, Hemsworth, Huddersfield, Rotherham, Sheffield, Wakefield

WREXHAM, DEN. (Holt, Hope, Ruabon)
Corwen, Ellesmere, Great Boughton, Holywell, Oswestry, Ruthin

WYCOMBE, BKM. (Great Marlow, High Wycombe, Princes Risborough, Wendover, West Wycombe)
Amersham, Aylesbury, Eton, Henley, Thame

YARMOUTH, NFK.
Blofield, Flegg, Mutford

YEOVIL, SOM. (Coker, Ilchester, Martock, South Petherton)
Bedminster, Chard, Langport, Sherborne, Wincanton

YORK, YKS. (Bootham, Dunnington, Escrick, Flaxton, Micklegate, Skelton, Walmgate)
Easingwold, Great Ouseburn, Howden, Kirk Deighton, Pocklington, Malton, Selby, Tadcaster, Wetherby

SUB-DISTRICTS

SUB-DISTRICT (Main District)

ABBEY (Bath)
ABBEY HULME (Wigton)
ABBOTS BROMLEY (Uttoxeter)
ABBOTS LANGLEY (Watford)
ABBOTSBURY (Weymouth)
ABERDARE (Merthyr Tydfil)
ABERDARON (Pwllheli)
ABERFORD (Tadcaster)
ABERGELE (St Asaph)
ABERWESSIN (Builth)
ABERYSTRUTH (Bedwelty)
ABTHORPE (Towcester)
ACCRINGTON (Haslingden)
ACTON (Brentford)
ADDINGHAM (Skipton)
ALBERBURY (Atcham)
ALBRIGHTON (Shifnal)
ALBURY (Guildford)
ALDBROUGH (Richmond YKS)
ALDBROUGH (Skirlaugh)
ALDEBOROUGH (Plomesgate)
ALDEBY (Loddon)
ALDERLEY (Macclesfield)
ALDGATE (Whitechapel)
ALDINGTON (East Ashford)
ALDRIDGE (Walsall)
ALFORD (Spilsby)
ALFRETON (Belper)
ALLENDALE (Hexham)
ALLERSTON (Pickering)
ALMONDBURY (Huddersfield)
ALMONDSBURY (Thornbury)
ALPHINGTON (St Thomas)
ALSTON (Preston)
ALTERNON (Launceston)
ALTON (Cheadle)
ALVERTHORPE (Wakefield)
AMBLESIDE (Kendal)
AMPORT (Andover)
AMROTH (Narberth)
ANCOATS (Manchester)
ANSTON (Worksop)
ANTONY (St Germans)
ANWELL (Clerkenwell)
APPLEBY (East Ward)
APPLETON ROEBUCK (Tadcaster)

APPLETON UPON WISKE
  (Northallerton)
ARDLEIGH (Tendring)
ARDSLEY (Wakefield)
ARDWICK (Chorlton)
ARKHOLME (Lancaster/Lunesdale)
ARNCLIFFE (Settle)
ARNOLD (Basford)
ARTILLERY (Whitechapel)
ARUNDEL (Worthing)
ASHBURTON (Newton Abbot)
ASHFORD (West Ashford)
ASHLEY (Clifton)
ASHOVER (Chesterfield)
ASLACKBY (Bourne)
ASPULL (Wigan)
ASTON CLINTON (Aylesbury)
ASTON MACKERFIELD (Wigan)
ASWARBY (Sleaford)
ATHERTON (Leigh)
ATTERCLIFFE (Sheffield)
ATTLEBOROUGH (Wayland)
AUDENSHAW (Ashton under Lyne)
AUDLEY (Newcastle under Lyme)
AUGHTON (Ormskirk)
AYCLIFFE (Darlington)
AYLESFORD (Malling)

BACTON (Tunstead)
BAINTON (Driffield)
BALDOCK (Hitchin)
BALSHAM (Linton)
BAMPTON (Tiverton)
BAMPTON (Witney)
BANHAM (Guiltcross)
BANWELL (Axbridge)
BARHAM (Bridge)
BARKING (Romford)
BARMBOROUGH (Doncaster)
BARNACK (Stamford)
BARNARD CASTLE (Teesdale)
BARNOLDSWICK (Skipton)
BARNWORTH (Dolgelly)
BARROWDEN (Uppingham)
BARTON (Glanford Brigg)
BASCHURCH (Ellesmere)

BASSINGHAM (Newark)
BATHEASTON (Bath)
BATHWICK (Bath)
BATLEY (Dewsbury)
BATTERSEA (Wandsworth)
BATTLEFIELD (Atcham)
BAWDESWELL (Mitford)
BAWTRY (Doncaster)
BEACONSFIELD (Amersham)
BEAUMARIS (Bangor)
BECCLES (Wangford)
BECKLEY (Rye)
BEDLINGTON (Morpeth)
BEGELLY (Narberth)
BEIGHTON (Rotherham)
BEILLY (Presteigne)
BELBROUGHTON (Bromsgrove)
BELGRAVE (St George Hanover
  Square)
BENNINGTON (Boston)
BENNINGTON (Newark)
BENTHAM (Settle)
BERE REGIS (Wareham)
BERKELEY (Thornbury)
BETTWS-Y-COED (Llanrwst)
BEWDLEY (Kidderminster)
BEXHILL (Battle)
BEXLEY (Dartford)
BIBERY (Northleach)
BICKERSTAFFE (Ormskirk)
BIDFORD (Alcester)
BILLINGHAY (Sleaford)
BILLINGHURST (Petworth)
BILLINGTON (Blackburn)
BILSTON (Wolverhampton)
BINBROOK (Louth)
BINGLEY (Keighley)
BINSTEAD (Alton)
BIRTLE (Bury)
BISHOP AUCKLAND (Auckland)
BISHOPS CANNING (Devizes)
BISHOPS CASTLE (Clun)
BISHOPS FROME (Bromyard)
BISHOPS LYDEARD (Taunton)
BISHOPS TAWTON (Barnstaple)
BISHOPS WALTHAM (Droxford)
BISHOPSTONE (Wilton)
BISLEY (Stroud)
BITTON (Keynsham)

BITTON (Tadcaster)
BLACK TORRINGTN (Holsworthy)
BLACKAWTON (Kingsbridge)
BLACKLEY (Manchester)
BLACKWELL (Mansfield)
BLAENAVON (Abergavenny)
BLAGDON (Axbridge)
BLATCHINWORTH (Rochdale)
BLETCHINGTON (Bicester)
BLIDWORTH (Mansfield)
BLOXHAM (Banbury)
BLOXWICH (Walsall)
BLYTH (Tynemouth)
BOBBINGWORTH (Ongar)
BOCKING (Braintree)
BOCKLETON (Tenbury)
BODENHAM (Leominster)
BOLLINGTON (Macclesfield)
BOLSOVER (Chesterfield)
BOOTHAM (York)
BOROUGHBRIDGE (Great
  Ousebourn)
BOSCASTLE (Camelford)
BOSTON (Wetherby)
BOTESDALE (Hartismere)
BOTTISHAM (Newmarket)
BOUGHTON (Faversham)
BOUGHTON (Stockbridge)
BOURTON ON THE WATER (Stow
  on the Wold)
BOW (Crediton)
BOW (Poplar)
BOWLING (Bradford)
BOXGROVE (Westhampnett)
BRABOURNE (East Ashford)
BRADFIELD (Wortley)
BRADFORD ABBAS (Sherborne)
BRADLEY (Westbury)
BRADWELL (Maldon)
BRADWORTH (Bideford)
BRAFIELD (Hardingstone)
BRAILSFORD (Ashborne)
BRAMHAM (Tadcaster)
BRAMLEY (Basingstoke)
BRANDESBURTON (Skirlaugh)
BRASSINGTON (Ashborne)
BRATTON CLOVELLY
  (Okehampton)
BRAUGHING (Bishop Stortford)

BRAUNTON (Barnstaple)
BRAY (Cookham)
BREAGE (Helston)
BRECKNELL (Easthampstead)
BRENCHLEY (Tunbridge)
BRENTWOOD (Billericay)
BRETTON (Wakefield)
BREWOOD (Penkridge)
BRIGG (Glanford Brigg)
BRIGHOUSE (Halifax)
BRIGHTSIDE (Sheffield
BRILL (Thame)
BRILLEY (Kington)
BRINDLE (Chorley)
BRITFORD (Alderbury)
BRIXHAM (Totnes)
BRIXTON (Lambeth)
BROAD CLIST (St Thomas)
BROADWATER (Worthing)
BROADWAY (Evesham)
BROADWOODWIDGER
   (Holsworthy)
BROCKHAMPTON (Bromyard)
BROMHAM (Devizes)
BROMPTON (Kensington)
BROSELEY (Madeley)
BROUGHTON (Preston)
BROUGHTON (Salford)
BRUTON (Wincanton)
BRYNGWAN (Anglesey)
BUBWITH (Howden)
BUCKFASTLEIGH (Totnes)
BUCKLAND (Faringdon)
BUCKLAND MONACHORUM
   (Tavistock)
BUCKLEBURY (Bradfield)
BUDBROOKE (Warwick)
BUDWORTH (Runcorn)
BUGBROOKE (Northampton)
BULMER (Malton)
BULMER (Sudbury)
BULWELL (Basford)
BUNBURY (Nantwich)
BUNGAY (Wangford)
BUNTINGFORD (Royston)
BURBAGE (Hinckley)
BURES (Sudbury)
BURFORD (Witney)
BURGH (Carlisle)

BURGH (Spilsby)
BURGHILL (Hereford)
BURNHAM (Axbridge)
BURNHAM (Docking)
BURNHAM (Eton)
BURSLEM (Wolstanton)
BURTON BRADSTOCK (Bridport)
BUSHEY (Watford)
BUTTERWORTH (Rochdale)
BUXTON (Aylsham)
BUXTON (Chapel en le Frith)
BYKER (Newcastle upon Tyne)
BYRON CASTLE (Nottingham)
BYWELL (Hexham)

CADOXTON (Neath)
CAERLEON (Newport MON)
CAERPHILLY (Cardiff)
CAINHAM (Ludlow)
CALBOURNE (Isle of Wight)
CALDBECK (Wigton)
CALEHILL (West Ashford)
CALLINGTON (Liskeard)
CALSTOCK (Tavistock)
CALTON (Ashborne)
CALVERLEY (Bradford)
CAMBORNE (Redruth)
CAMDEN TOWN (Pancras)
CAMPSALL (Doncaster)
CANFORD (Poole)
CANNOCK (Penkridge)
CAPEL (Dorking)
CAPEL ST MARY (Samford)
CARBURTON (Worksop)
CARDINGTON (Bedford)
CARLFORD (Woodbridge)
CARLTON (Basford)
CARLTON (Selby)
CARLTON (Worksop)
CARSHALTON (Epsom)
CARTMEL (Ulverston)
CASTLE CARY (Wincanton)
CASTLE CHURCH (Stafford)
CASTLE COMBE (Chippenham)
CASTLE DONINGTON (Shardlow)
CASTLE RISING (Freebridge Lynn)
CASTLEFORD (Pontefract)
CASTLETON (Rochdale)
CATON (Lancaster/Lunesdale)

CATTERICK (Richmond YKS)
CAWTHORPE (Wortley)
CERNE (Dorchester)
CHADDERSLEY-CORBETT
 (Kidderminster)
CHADDERTON (Oldham)
CHAGFORD (Okehampton)
CHAILEY (Lewes)
CHALFONT (Amersham)
CHAPELTOWN (Hunslet/Leeds)
CHARDSTOCK (Axminster)
CHARING CROSS (St Martin in the
 Fields)
CHARLBURY (Chipping Norton)
CHARLTON KINGS (Cheltenham)
CHARTHAM (Bridge)
CHATTERIS (NorthWitchford)
CHEADLE (Stockport)
CHEDWORTH (Northleach)
CHEETHAM (Manchester)
CHERITON (Crediton)
CHESHAM (Amersham)
CHESHUNT (Edmonton)
CHETTON (Bridgnorth)
CHEVELEY (Newmarket)
CHEW MAGNA (Clutton)
CHIGWELL (Epping)
CHIPPING (Clitheroe)
CHIPPING ONGAR (Ongar)
CHIRBURY (Montgomery)
CHISLEHURST (Bromley)
CHISWICK (Brentford)
CHOBHAM (Chertsey)
CHOLLERTON (Hexham)
CHOLSEY (Wallingford)
CHRISTIAN MALFORD
 (Chippenham)
CHRISTOW (St Thomas)
CHUDLEIGH (Newton Abbot)
CHULMLEIGH (South Molton)
CHURCH HOLME (Congleton)
CILYCWM (Llandovery)
CITY ROAD (St Luke)
CLAINES (Droitwich)
CLAPHAM (Wandsworth)
CLARBOROUGH (East Retford)
CLARE (Risbridge)
CLAWSON (Melton Mowbray)
CLAWTON (Holsworthy)

CLAYPOLE (Newark)
CLEARS (Carmarthen)
CLECKHEATON (Bradford)
CLEEVE (Winchcomb)
CLODOCK (Hereford)
CLOWANCE (Stoke Damerel)
CLYRO (Hay)
CODDENHAM (Bosmere)
COGGLESHALL (Witham)
COKER (Yeovil)
COLEFORD (Monmouth)
COLESHILL (Meriden)
COLLINGBOURNE (Pewsey)
COLNE (Burnley)
COLNESS (Woodbridge)
COLSTERWORTH (Grantham)
COLTON (Ulverston)
COLWICH (Stafford)
COLWYN (Builth)
COLYTON (Axminster)
COMBE ST NICHOLAS (Chard)
COMBMARTIN (Barnstaple)
CONDOVER (Atcham)
CONIFORD (Norwich)
CONSTANTINE (Falmouth)
CONWIL (Carmarthen)
CONWIL GAYO (Llandovery)
CORBY (Bourne)
CORBY (Kettering)
CORFE CASTLE (Wareham)
CORSHAM (Chippenham)
COSLANY (Norwich)
COSTESSEY (Forehoe)
COTINGHAM (Sculcoates)
COTSWOLD (Cirencester)
COWBRIDGE (Bridgend)
COWES (Isle of Wight)
COXWOLD (Easingwold)
CRANBORNE (Wimborne)
CRANFIELD (Ampthill)
CRANLEY (Hambledon)
CREUDDYN (Conway)
CREWKERNE (Chard)
CRICCIETH (Pwllheli)
CRICK (Rugby)
CROMER (Erpington)
CROMPTON (Oldham)
CROPREDY (Banbury)
CROSBY (West Derby)

CROSTON (Chorley)
CROWAN (Helston)
CROWLAND (Peterborough)
CROWLE (Thorne)
CULCHETH (Leigh)
CULLAMPTON (Tiverton)
CULMSTOCK (Wellington SOM)
CUMNOR (Abingdon)
CURREY-RIVELL (Langport)
CWMDU (Crickhowell)

DACRE BANKS (Pateley Bridge)
DALSTON (Carlisle)
DALTON (Ulverston)
DANBURY (Guisborough)
DARESBURY (Runcorn)
DARFIELD (Barnsley)
DARLASTON (Walsall)
DAROWEN (Machynlleth)
DARTMOUTH (Totnes)
DARTON (Barnsley)
DARWEN (Blackburn)
DAWLEY (Madeley)
DEAL (Eastry)
DEANSGATE (Manchester)
DEDDINGTON (Woodstock)
DEDHAM (Lexden)
DEEPING (Bourne)
DEEPING ST NICHOLAS (Spalding)
DEERHURST (Tewkesbury)
DELPH (Saddleworth)
DENBIGH (St Asaph)
DENNINGTON (Hoxne)
DENT (Sedburgh)
DENTON (Ashton under Lyne)
DENTON (Grantham)
DEPTFORD (Woolwich)
DERITEND (Aston)
DEVYNNOCK (Brecknock)
DEWCHURCH (Hereford)
DIDDLESBURY (Ludlow)
DIDMARTON (Tetbury)
DIDSBURY (Chorlton)
DILHORNE (Cheadle)
DILWYN (Weobly)
DINGESTOW (Monmouth)
DISHFORTH (Ripon)
DISS (Depwade)
DITCHLING (Lewes)

DOLTON (Torrington)
DONHEAD (Tisbury)
DONINGTON (Spalding)
DOWNTON (Alderbury)
DRIGLINGTON (Bradford)
DRONFIELD (Chesterfield)
DRYPOOL (Sculcoates)
DUCKINFIELD (Ashton under Lyne)
DUDDESTON (Aston)
DUFFIELD (Belper)
DULWICH (Camberwell)
DUMMER (Basingstoke)
DUNCHURCH (Rugby)
DUNNINGTON (York)
DUNSTABLE (Luton)
DUNSTER (Williton)
DUXFORD (Linton)

EARL SHILTON (Hinckley)
EARL SOHAM (Plomesgate)
EARLS BARTON (Wellingborough)
EARSDON (Tynemouth)
EAST BUDLEIGH (St Thomas)
EAST DEREHAM (Mitford)
EAST MEON (Petersfield)
EAST PECKHAM (Malling)
EAST STAMFORD BRIDGE
    (Pocklington)
EAST WYMER (Norwich)
EASTCHURCH (Sheppey)
EASTHAM (Wirral)
ECCLESFIELD (Wortley)
ECCLESHALL (Stone)
ECKINGTON (Chesterfield)
ECKINGTON (Pershore)
EDDLESBOROUGH (Leighton
    Buzzard)
EDENFIELD (Haslingden)
EDGBASTON (Kings Norton)
EDGEWORTH (Bolton)
EDGWARE (Hendon)
EDINGTON (Westbury)
EGHAM (Windsor)
EGLOSHAYLE (Bodmin)
EGREMONT (Whitehaven)
EGTON (Whitby)
ELING (New Forest)
ELLAND (Halifax)
ELLEL (Lancaster)

ELSDON (Rothbury)
ELTHAM (Lewisham)
ELTON (Bury)
EMBLETON (Alnwick)
ENDERBY (Blaby)
ENFIELD (Edmonton)
ENSHAM (Witney)
EPWORTH (Thorne)
ERCALL MAGNA (Wellington SAL)
ERDINGTON (Aston)
ESCRICK (York)
ESHER (Kingston)
EVERCREECH (Shepton Mallet)
EVERSHOT (Beaminster)
EVERTON (West Derby)
EWHURST (Battle)
EXCHANGE (Nottingham)
EXMOUTH (St Thomas)
EYE (Hartismere)
EYNSFORD (Aylsham)
EYTHORN (Eastry)

FAILSWORTH (Manchester)
FAIRFORD (Cirencester)
FAKENHAM (Walsingham)
FARNBOROUGH (Hartley Wintney)
FARNINGHAM (Dartford)
FARNWORTH (Bolton)
FARNWORTH (Prescot)
FAWLEY (New Forest)
FAZELEY (Tamworth)
FECKENHAM (Alcester)
FENNY STRATFORD (Newport
  Pagnell)
FENTON (Stoke on Trent)
FERNHURST Midhurst)
FERRYBY (Sculcoates)
FEWSTON (Wharfedale)
FILEY (Scarborough)
FINCHAM (Downham)
FINCHINGFIELD (Braintree)
FINCHLEY (Barnet)
FINSBURY (St Luke)
FISHGUARD (Haverfordwest)
FITZPAINE (Crediton)
FLAMSTEAD (Hemel Hempstead)
FLAXTON (York)
FLINT (Holywell)
FOLKESTONE (Elham)

FONTMELL (Shaftesbury)
FORD (Glendale)
FORDHAM (Lexden)
FORMBY (Ormskirk)
FORNCETT (Depwade)
FORNHAM (Thingoe)
FOSTON (Driffield)
FOTHERINGHAY (Oundle)
FOWEY (St Austell)
FOWNHOPE (Hereford)
FRAMFIELD (Uckfield)
FRAMLINGHAM (Plomesgate)
FRAMPTON (Wheatenhurst)
FRANT (Ticehurst)
FRIMLEY (Farnham)
FRODSHAM (Runcorn)
FULBOURN (Chesterton)
FULHAM (Kensington)
FUNTINGTON (Westbourne)
FYFIELD (Abingdon)

GARGRAVE (Skipton)
GARSDALE (Sedburgh)
GAWSWORTH (Macclesfield)
GAYTON (Freebridge Lynn)
GAZELEY (Newmarket)
GEDNEY HILL (Holbeach)
GELLIGAER (Merthyr Tydfil)
GENEURGLYNN (Aberystwyth)
GILDERSOME (Bramley)
GILLINGHAM (Medway)
GILLINGHAM (Shaftesbury)
GISBURN (Clitheroe)
GLASTONBURY (Wells)
GLOSSOP (Hayfield)
GNOSALL (Newport SAL)
GODSHILL (Isle of Wight)
GOLCAR (Huddersfield)
GOLDALMING (Guildford)
GOMERSALL (Dewsbury)
GORLESTON (Mutford)
GOSBERTON (Spalding)
GOSWELL STREET (Clerkenwell)
GRAMPOUND (St Austell)
GRASSINGTON (Skipton)
GRAYRIGG (Kendal)
GRAYS (Orsett)
GREASLEY (Basford)
GREAT BADDOW (Chelmsford)

GREAT BURSTEAD (Billericay)
GREAT EASTON (Uppingham)
GREAT GRIMSBY (Caistor)
GREAT MARLOW (Wycombe)
GREAT SHELFORD (Chesterton)
GREAT WAKERING (Rochford)
GREAT WALTHAM (Chelmsford)
GREENGATE (Salford)
GRESLEY (Burton Trent)
GREYSTOKE (Penrith)
GRINGLEY (East Retford)
GUITING (Winchcomb)
GWENNAP (Redruth)
GWYDDELWERN (Corwen)
GWYNNWS (Tregaron)
GYFFYLLIOG (Ruthin)

HADDENHAM (Aylesbury)
HADDENHAM (Ely)
HADLEIGH (Cosford)
HAGGERSTON (Shoreditch)
HALE (Prescot)
HALESOWEN (Stourbridge)
HALESWORTH (Blything)
HALFORD (Shipston on Stour)
HALLIWELL (Bolton)
HALSALL (Ormskirk)
HAMBLEDON (Droxford)
HAMMERSMITH (Kensington)
HAMPSTEAD (Newton Abbot)
HAMPTON (Kingston)
HAMSTERLEY (Auckland)
HANDSWORTH (Sheffield)
HANDSWORTH (West Bromwich)
HANLEY (Stoke on Trent)
HANLEY (Upton Severn)
HANMER (Ellesmere)
HARBERTON (Totnes)
HARBORNE (Kings Norton)
HARESFIELD (Wheatenhurst)
HAREWOOD (Otley)
HARLESTON (Depwade)
HARLOW (Epping)
HARPENDEN (St Albans)
HARPTREE (Clutton)
HARRATON (Chester-le-Street)
HARRINGTON (Whitehaven)
HARROGATE (Knaresborough)
HARROLD (Bedford)

HARROW (Hendon)
HARTEST (Sudbury)
HARTING (Midhurst)
HARTINGTON (Ashborne)
HARTLAND (Bideford)
HARTSHEAD (Ashton under Lyne)
HARTSHORN (Ashby de la Zouch)
HARWICH (Tendring)
HARWOOD (Blackburn)
HATFIELD (Dunmow)
HATHERLEIGH (Okehampton)
HAVERHILL (Risbridge)
HAWARDEN (Great Boughton)
HAWES (Askrigg)
HAWKESBURY (Chipping Sodbury)
HAWKESHEAD (Ulverston)
HAWKHURST (Cranbrook)
HAWORTH (Keighley)
HAYES (Uxbridge)
HAYTON (Brampton)
HAZEL GROVE (Stockport)
HEADCORN (Hollingbourn)
HEADLEY (Farnborough)
HEATON (Lancaster)
HEATON NORRIS (Stockport)
HEAVITREE (St Thomas)
HEBDEN BRIDGE (Todmorden)
HECKINGTON (Sleaford)
HEDINGTON (Halstead)
HEDON (Sculcoates)
HELLINGLY (Hailsham)
HENDRED (Wantage)
HERNE (Blean)
HESSLE (Sculcoates)
HETTON LE HOLE (Houghton le
    Spring)
HEWORTH (Gateshead)
HEYTESBURY (Warminster)
HEYWOOD (Bury)
HIGH BICKINGTON (Torrington)
HIGH HOYLAND (Wortley)
HIGH LONGTOWN (Longtown)
HIGH WYCOMBE (Wycombe)
HIGHAM FERRERS (Wellingborough)
HIGHCLERE (Kingsclere)
HILLINGDON (Uxbridge)
HILLINGTON (Freebridge Lynn)
HINDLEY (Wigan)
HINDON (Tisbury)

HODDESTON (Ware)
HODNEY (Market Drayton)
HOLBECK (Hunslet)
HOLBROOK (Samford)
HOLCOMBE (Bury)
HOLME (Howden)
HOLMFIRTH (Huddersfield)
HOLT (Erpingham)
HOLT (Martley)
HOLT (Wrexham)
HOLYHEAD (Anglesey)
HOLYWELL (Shoreditch)
HONLEY (Huddersfield)
HOPE (Wrexham)
HORBURY (Wakefield)
HORLEY (Reigate)
HORNCHURCH (Romford)
HORNDEAN (Catherington)
HORNSEA (Skirlaugh)
HORNSEY (Edmonton)
HORSFORTH (Wharfedale)
HORSLEY (Belper)
HORSLEY (Stroud)
HORTON (Bradfield)
HORWICH (Bolton)
HOUGHAM (Dover)
HOVINGHAM (Malton)
HOXTON (Shoreditch)
HULME (Chorlton)
HULTON (Bolton)
HUMBER (Hull)
HUMBLETON (Skirlaugh)
HUMBLEYARD (Henstead)
HUNTLEY (Westbury on Severn)
HUNTSPILL (Bridgewater)
HURSLEY (Winchester)
HURSTBOURNE TARRANT
  (Andover)
HURSTPIERPOINT (Cuckfield)
HUTTON (Stokesley)
HUTTON-BUSHELL (Scarborough)
HUXMANBY (Bridlington)
HUYTON (Prescot)
HYDE (Stockport)
HYSON GREEN (Radford)
HYTHE (Elham)

IBSTOCK (Market Bosworth)
IDLE (Bradford)

ILCHESTER (Yeovil)
ILFORD (Romford)
ILFRACOMBE (Barnstaple)
ILKESTON (Basford)
ILLOGEN (Redruth)
ILMINSTER (Chard)
ILSLEY (Wantage)
INGATESTONE (Chelmsford)
IPSTONES (Cheadle)
IRON ACTON (Chipping Sodbury)
ISFIELD (Uckfield)
ISLANDSHIRE (Berwick)
ISLEWORTH (Brentford)
IVER (Eton)
IVINGHOE (Leighton Buzzard)
IXWORTH (Thingoe)

KEA (Truro)
KELVENDON (Witham)
KEMPSEY (Upton upon Severn)
KEMPSTON (Bedford)
KENARTH (Newcastle in Emlyn)
KENILWORTH (Warwick)
KENNINGHALL (Guiltcross)
KENNINGTON (Lambeth)
KENTCHURCH (Hereford)
KENTISH TOWN (Pancras)
KENTON (St Thomas)
KENWYN (Truro)
KERRY (Newtown)
KESSINGLAND (Mutford)
KESWICK (Cockermouth)
KETTLEWELL (Skipton)
KILDWICK (Skipton)
KILKHAMPTON (Stratton)
KILMERSDON (Frome)
KIMBERLEY (Rotherham)
KIMBOLTON (St Neots)
KINETON (Stratford on Avon)
KINFARE (Wolverhampton)
KINGS LANGLEY (Hemel
  Hempstead)
KINGSHOLM (Gloucester)
KINGSLAND (Leominster)
KINGSTON (Portsea Island)
KINGSWINFORD (Stourbridge)
KINGTON (Presteigne)
KINSHAM (Kington)
KINTBURY (Hungerford)

KIPPAX (Pontefract)
KIRK-LEATHAM (Guisborough)
KIRKBURTON (Huddersfield)
KIRKBY (East Ward)
KIRKBY (Settle)
KIRKBY LONSDALE (Kendal)
KIRKBY MALZEARD (Ripon)
KIRKBY MOORSIDE (Helmsly)
KIRKDALE (West Derby)
KIRKHAM (Fylde)
KIRKHEATON (Huddersfield)
KIRKOSWALD (Penrith)
KIRKSTALL (Hunslet)
KIRKSTALL (Leeds)
KIRKWHELPNGHAM (Bellingham)
KIRTON HOLLAND (Boston)
KNAYTON (Thirsk)
KNEESAL (Southwell)
KNOCKIN (Oswestry)
KNOTTINGLEY (Pontefract)
KNOTTS LANES (Ashton under Lyne)
KNOWLE (Solihull)
KNUTSFORD (Altrincham)

LAKENHEATH (Mildenhall)
LAMBOURN (Hungerford)
LANCHESTER (Durham)
LANDPORT (Portsea Island)
LANGTOFT (Driffield)
LANLIVERY (Bodmin)
LANSDOWN (Bath)
LASTINGHAM (Pickering)
LATHOM (Ormskirk)
LAVENHAM (Cosford)
LAVINGTON (Devizes)
LEADENHAM (Sleaford
LEAKE (Loughborough)
LEAMINGTON (Warwick)
LEATHERHEAD (Epsom)
LECKHAMPSTEAD (Buckingham)
LEE (Lewisham)
LEIGH (Martley)
LEINTWARDINE (Ludlow)
LENHAM (Hollingbourn)
LENTON (Radford)
LERRIN (Liskeard)
LETCHFORD (Warrington)
LEVEN (Beverley)

LEVER (Bolton)
LEVERINGTON (Wisbech)
LEWKNOR (Thame)
LEYLAND (Chorley)
LEYTON (West Ham)
LIFTON (Tavistock)
LIMEHOUSE (Stepney)
LINDFIELD (Cuckfield)
LITEHAM (Mitford)
LITHERLAND (West Derby)
LITTLEHAMPTON (Worthing)
LITTLEPORT (Ely)
LIVERSEDGE (Dewsbury)
LLANARMON (Ruthin)
LLANARTH (Abergavenny)
LLANBISTER (Knighton)
LLANBOIDY (Narberth)
LLANBYTHER (Lampeter)
LLANDDAUSAINT (Llandovery)
LLANDEBIE (Llanilofawr)
LLANDILO (Llanilofawr)
LLANDILOTALYBONT (Swansea)
LLANDINGAT (Llandovery)
LLANDISILIO (Aberayron)
LLANDISILIO (Narberth)
LLANDWROG (Caernarvon)
LLANDYFRYDOG (Anglesey)
LLANDYGWYDD (Cardigan)
LLANDYRNOG (Ruthin)
LLANDYSSIL (Lampeter)
LLANDYSSIL (Newcastle in Emlyn)
LLANELIDAN (Ruthin)
LLANELLY (Crickhowell)
LLANFAIR (Llanfyllin)
LLANFAIRARYBRYN (Llandovery)
LLANFIHANGELYTRAETHAU (Festiniog)
LLANFYNYDD (Llanilofawr)
LLANGADOCK (Llandovery)
LLANGATELACH (Swansea)
LLANGATHEN (Llanilofawr)
LLANGATTOCK (Crickhowel)
LLANGEFNI (Anglesey)
LLANGEITHO (Tregaron)
LLANGENDEIRNE (Carmarth)
LLANGIBBY (Pontypool)
LLANGOLLEN (Corwen)
LLANGORSE (Brecknock)
LLANGUNIDER (Crickhowel)

LLANIDAN (Carnarvon)
LLANIDLOES (Newtown)
LLANLLECHID (Bangor)
LLANNON (Llanelly)
LLANRHAIADR (Llanfyllin)
LLANRHAIADR (Ruthin)
LLANRHYSTYD (Aberystwyth)
LLANRUG (Carnarvon)
LLANSADWEN (Llandovery)
LLANSAINTFFRAID (Aberayron)
LLANSAINTFFRAID (Llanfyllin)
LLANSAMLET (Neath)
LLANSILIN (Oswestry)
LLANTRISAINT (Cardiff)
LLANTRISAINT (Pontypridd)
LLANVILHANGEL (Abergavenny)
LLANWNOG (Newtown)
LLANWRTYD (Llandovery)
LOCKINGTON (Beverley)
LOCKTON (Pickering)
LOCKWOOD (Huddersfield)
LOFTHOUSE (Guisborough)
LONDON ROAD (Manchester)
LONG ACRE (St Martin in the Fields)
LONG ASHTON (Bedminster)
LONG BEATON (Tynemouth)
LONG BUCKLEY (Daventry)
LONG PRESTON (Settle)
LONG SUTTON (Holbeach)
LONGBRIDGE-DEVERILL (Warminster)
LONGNOT (Leek)
LONGPARISH (Andover)
LONGTON (Preston)
LONGTON (Stoke on Trent)
LOOE (Liskeard)
LOOSE (Maidstone)
LOUGHOR (Llanelly)
LOW LONGTOWN (Longtown)
LOWER MITTON (Kidderminster)
LOWESTOFT (Mutford)
LOWTHER (West Ward)
LOWTON (Leigh)
LUDDENHAM (Halifax)
LUDGERSHALL (Andover)
LUDHAM (Tunstead)
LYDD (Romney Marsh)
LYDNEY (Chepstow)

LYME (Axminster)
LYMM (Altrincham)
LYNCOMBE (Bath)
LYNDHURST (New Forest)
LYTCHETT (Poole)
LYTHAM (Fylde)
LYTHE (Whitby)

MADLEY (Hereford)
MAESTEG (Bridgend)
MAIDEN NEWTON (Dorchstr)
MALHAM (Settle)
MALPAS (Whitchurch SAL)
MALTBY (Rotherham)
MANCROFT (Norwich)
MANHOOD (Westhampnett)
MANNINGTREE (Tendring)
MARAZION (Penzance)
MARCH (North Witchford)
MARDEN (Maidstone)
MARESFIELD (Uckfield)
MARGAM (Neath)
MARGATE (Thanet)
MARKET RASEN (Caistor)
MARKET STREET (Manchester)
MARKET WEIGHTON (Pocklington)
MARPLE (Stockport)
MARSHFIELD (Chipping Sodbury)
MARSKE (Guisborough)
MARTOCK (Yeovil)
MARTON (Gainsborough)
MARYPORT (Cockermouth)
MASHAM (Bedale)
MATLOCK (Bakewell)
MATTISHALL (Mitford)
MAYFIELD (Ashborne)
MEASHAM (Ashby de la Zouch)
MELBOURN (Royston)
MELBOURNE (Shardlow)
MELFORD (Sudbury)
MELLOR (Blackburn)
MELTHAM (Huddersfield)
MENDLESHAM (Hartismere)
MERTHYR CYNOG (Brecknock)
METHWOLD (Thetford)
MEVAGISSEY (St Austell)
MICHELMERSH (Romsey)
MICKLEGATE (York)
MIDDLEHAM (Leyburn)

MIDDLETON (Freebridge Lynn)
MIDDLETON (Oldham)
MIDDLETON (Teesdale)
MIDDLEWICH (Northwich)
MIDDLEZOY (Bridgewater)
MIDSOMER NORTON (Clutton)
MILBORNE PORT (Wincanton)
MILFORD (Haverfordwest)
MILFORD (Lymington)
MILLBROOK (South Stoneham)
MILNTHORPE (Kendal)
MILTON (Hardingstone)
MILTON ABBAS (Blandford)
MILTON ABBOT (Tavistock)
MILTON DAMEREL
 (Bideford/Holsworthy)
MILVERTON (Wellington SOM)
MINCHINHAMPTON (Stroud)
MINEHEAD (Williton)
MINSTER (Sheppey)
MINSTER (Thanet)
MIRFIELD (Dewsbury)
MISSENDEN (Amersham)
MISTERTON (Beaminster)
MISTERTON (Gainsborough)
MITCHAM (Croydon)
MITCHELDEVER (Winchester)
MODBURY (Kingsbridge)
MOLD (Holywell)
MONKWEARMOUTH (Sunderland)
MONTFORD (Atcham)
MORCHARD BISHOP (Crediton)
MORETON (Newton Abbot)
MORETON (Shipston on Stour)
MORETON SAY (Market Drayton)
MORICE (Stoke Damerel)
MORLAND (West Ward)
MORLEY (Dewsbury)
MORTIMER (Bradfield)
MORTLAKE (Richmond SRY)
MOTTRAM (Ashton under Lyne)
MOULTON (Brixworth)
MOULTON (Spalding)
MUCH WENLOCK (Madeley)
MUCH WOOLTON (Prescot)
MUKER (Reeth)
MUNCASTER (Bootle)
MUNSLOW (Ludlow)
MYDDFAI (Llandovery)

MYLOR (Falmouth)
MYNYDDYSLWYN (Newport MON)
MYTON (Hull)

NANTMEL (Rhayader)
NEEDHAM MARKET (Bosmere)
NESTON (Wirral)
NETHER HALLAM (Ecclesall
 Bierlow)
NETHERAVON (Pewsey)
NETHERBURY (Beaminster)
NEVIN (Pwllheli)
NEW ROMNEY (Romney Marsh)
NEWCHURCH (Haslingden)
NEWHAVEN (Lewes)
NEWLYN (St Columb)
NEWMILL (Huddersfield)
NEWNHAM (Westbury on Severn)
NEWPORT (Cardigan)
NEWPORT (Howden)
NEWPORT (Isle of Wight)
NEWPORT (Saffron Walden)
NEWSHAM (Richmond YKS)
NEWTON (Ashton Lyne)
NEWTON (Keynsham)
NEWTON (Manchester)
NEWTON IN MACKERFIELD
 (Warrington)
NORBURY (Clun)
NORHAMSHIRE (Berwick)
NORTH BIERLEY (Bradford)
NORTH BISHOPSWEARMOUTH
 (Sunderland)
NORTH COLLINGHAM (Newark)
NORTH CURRY (Taunton)
NORTH ELMHAM (Mitford)
NORTH LYDBURY (Clun)
NORTH MEOLS (Ormskirk)
NORTH PETERWIN (Launceston)
NORTH PETHERTON (Bridgewater)
NORTH SHIELDS (Tynemth)
NORTH TAWTON (Okehampton)
NORTH WALSHAM (Erpingham)
NORTHAM (Bideford)
NORTHFLEET (North Aylesford)
NORTHILL (Launceston)
NORTHOWRAM (Halifax)
NORTON (Ecclesall Bierlow)
NORTON (Leek)

NORWOOD (Lambeth)
NUNEHAM COURTNEY
(Abingdon)
NUNNEY (Frome)

ODIHAM (Hartley Wintney)
OLD STRATFORD (Stratford on
Avon)
OLD STREET (St Luke)
OLDBURY (West Bromwich)
OLDLAND (Keynsham)
OLNEY (Newport Pagnell)
OMBERSLEY (Droitwich)
ORCHESTON (Amesbury)
ORE (Hastings)
ORFORD (Plomesgate)
ORMESBY (Middlesbrough)
OSSETT (Dewsbury)
OSWALDKIRK (Helmsley)
OTTERY ST MARY (Honiton)
OULTON (Wakefield)
OVENDON (Halifax)
OVER (Northwich)
OVERBURY (Tewkesbury)
OVERTON (Ellesmere)
OWSTON (Gainsborough)

PADDINGTON (Kensington)
PADIHAM (Burnley)
PADSTOW (St Columb)
PAIGNTON (Totnes)
PAINSWICK (Stroud)
PARACOMBE (Barnstaple)
PARK (Nottingham)
PARKHAM (Bideford)
PECKHAM (Camberwell)
PELDON (Lexden)
PEMBERTON (Wigan)
PEMBURY (Llanelly)
PENBRYN (Lampeter)
PENBRYN (Newcastle in Emlyn)
PENDLE (Burnley)
PENDLETON (Salford)
PENISTONE (Wortley)
PENKELLY (Brecknock)
PENNAL (Machynlleth)
PENRYN (Falmouth)
PENSHURST (Sevenoaks)
PENTONVILLE (Clerkenwell)

PHILLACK (Redruth)
PICKHILL (Thirsk)
PILKINGTON (Bury)
PINCHBECK (Spalding)
PITMINSTER (Taunton)
PLEASEY (Mansfield)
PLUMSTEAD (Lewisham/Woolwich)
POLDEN HILL (Bridgewater)
PONTELAND (Castle Ward)
PONTERSBURY (Atcham)
POOL (Montgomery)
POPPLETON (Great Ouseburn)
PORTLAND (Weymouth)
PORTSMOUTH (Portsea Island)
POTTON (Biggleswade)
POULTON LE FYLDE (Fylde)
PREES (Wem)
PRESTEIGNE (Knighton)
PRESTWICH (Manchester)
PRINCES RISBOROUGH (Wycombe)
PRITTLESWELL (Rochford)
PROBUS (Truro)
PUDDLETOWN (Dorchester)
PUDSEY (Bradford)
PULBOROUGH (Thakeham)
PUTNEY (Wandsworth)

QUERDON (Barrow on Soar)

RADCLIFFE (Bury)
RADFORD (Warwick)
RADNOR (Kington)
RADNOR (Presteigne)
RADWINTER (Saffron Waldon)
RAINFORD (Prescot)
RAINOW (Macclesfield)
RAMSEY (Huntingdon)
RAMSGATE (Thanet)
RAMSGILL (Pateley Bridge)
RASTRICK (Halifax)
RATCLIFF (Stepney)
RATCLIFFE ON TRENT (Bingham)
RATTLESDEN (Stow)
RAUNDS (Thrapston)
RAYLEIGH (Rochford)
REDMARLEY (Newent)
REGENT ROAD (Salford)
REPTON (Burton on Trent)
RHEIDOL (Aberystwyth)

RICCALL (Selby)
RICKMANSWORTH (Watford)
RILLINGTON (Malton)
RIPLEY (Belper)
RIPLEY (Guildford)
RIPPONDEN (Halifax)
RISELEY (Bedford)
RIVINGTON (Chorley)
RIXTON (Warrington)
ROAD (Frome)
ROCHESTER (Medway)
ROCK (Bedwellty)
RODBOROUGH (Stroud)
ROLVENDEN (Tenterden)
ROOSE (Pembroke)
ROPLEY (Alresford)
ROSSENDALE (Haslingden)
ROTHERFIELD (Uckfield)
ROTHLEY (Barrow on Soar)
ROTHWELL (Hunslet)
ROTHWELL (Kettering)
ROTTINGDEAN (Lewes)
ROUGHAM (Thingoe)
ROWLEY REGIS (Dudley)
ROYTON (Oldham)
RUABON (Wrexham)
RUGELEY (Lichfield)
RYDE (Isle of Wight)

SAHAM-TONEY (Swaffham)
ST AGNES (Truro)
ST AUBYN (Stoke Damerel)
ST BEES (Whitehaven)
ST BURYAN (Penzance)
ST CLEMENT (Truro)
ST CLEMENTS (Headington)
ST DAVIDS (Haverfordwest)
ST GEORGE (Camberwell)
ST GEORGE (Bedminster)
ST GEORGE (Manchester)
ST HELENS (Prescot)
ST IVES (Penzance)
ST JAMES (Clerkenwell)
ST JOHN (Weardale)
ST JUST (Truro)
ST JUST IN PENWITH (Penzance)
ST KEVERNE (Helston)
ST LEONARD (Shoreditch)
ST MABYN (Bodmin)

ST MARY (Hull)
ST MARY EXTRA (South Stoneham)
ST MICHAEL WYRE (Garstang)
ST NICHOLAS (Durham)
ST NICHOLAS (Cardiff)
ST OSWALD (Durham)
ST OSYTH (Tendring)
ST STEPHENS (Launceston)
ST WEONARDS (Ross)
ST WOOLLOS (Newport MON)
SALEHURST (Ticehurst)
SALTASH (St Germans)
SALTFLEET (Louth)
SANDAL (Wakefield)
SANDBACH (Congleton)
SANDWICH (Eastry)
SANKEY (Warrington)
SAWTRY (Huntingdon)
SAXMUNDHAM (Plomesgate)
SCARISBROOKE (Ormskirk)
SCOTTER (Gainsborough)
SEDGEFIELD (Stockton)
SEDGLEY (Dudley)
SHADWELL (Stepney)
SHARNBROOK (Bedford)
SHARPLES (Bolton)
SHEBBEAR (Torrington)
SHELTON (Stoke on Trent)
SHERBURN (Scarborough)
SHERWOOD (Nottingham)
SHILLINGFORD (Ampthill)
SHIPDHAM (Mitford)
SHIPLEY (Bradford)
SHIRE NEWTON (Chepstow)
SHOREHAM (Sevenoaks)
SHOREHAM (Steyning)
SHRIVENHAM (Faringdon)
SIBSEY (Boston)
SILVERTON (Tiverton)
SINGLETON (Westhampnett)
SINNINGTON (Pickering)
SKELTON (York)
SKIPSEA (Bridlington)
SLAIDBURN (Clitheroe)
SLAITHWAITE (Huddersfield)
SMALLBURGH (Tunstead)
SNAITH (Goole)
SNENTON (Radford)
SNETTISHAM (Docking)

SOLLERSHOPE (Ross)
SOMERBY (Melton Mowbray)
SOMERSHAM (St Ives)
SOMERTON (Langport)
SOOTHILL (Dewsbury)
SOUTH BERSTED (Chichester)
SOUTH BISHOPSWEARMOUTH
  (Sunderland)
SOUTH CAVE (Beverley)
SOUTH HAMLET (Gloucester)
SOUTH MIMMS (Barnet)
SOUTH PETHERTON (Yeovil)
SOUTH WALSHAM (Blofield)
SOUTHMINSTER (Maldon)
SOUTHOWRAM (Halifax)
SOWE (Foleshill)
SOWERBY (Halifax)
SPALDWICK (Huntingdon)
SPEEN (Newbury)
SPITALFIELDS (Whitechapel)
SPONDON (Shardlow)
SPOTLAND (Rochdale)
SPRATTON (Brixworth)
SPROWSTON (St Faiths)
STAINDROP (Teesdale)
STALBRIDGE (Sturminster)
STALHAM (Tunstead)
STALMINE (Garstang)
STAMFORD HILL (Hackney)
STAMFORDHAM (Castle Ward)
STANDISH (Wigan)
STANDON (Ware)
STANHOPE (Weardale)
STANLEY (Wakefield)
STANSTEAD (Ware)
STANSTED (Bishop Stortford)
STANWAY (Lexden)
STANWIX (Carlisle)
STAPLEFORD (Shardlow)
STAPLETON (Clifton)
STAYLEY (Ashton under Lyne)
STEBBING (Dunmow)
STEPHEN ORTON (East Ward)
STICKNEY (Spilsby)
STILLINGTON (Easingwold)
STILTON (Peterborough)
STOGUMBER (Williton)
STOGURSEY (Williton)
STOKE (Stoke Damerel)

STOKE LANE (Shepton Mallet)
STOKE NEWINGTON (Hackney)
STOKENHAM (Kingsbridge)
STONEHOUSE (Stroud)
STOTTESDEN (Cleobury Mortimer)
STOUR CAMPDEN (Shipston)
STOWEY (Bridgewater)
STOWMARKET (Stow)
STRADBROKE (Hoxne)
STRATFORD (West Ham)
STRATTON (Depwade)
STREATHAM (Wandsworth)
STRETFORD (Barton Irwel)
STROOD (North Aylesford)
STUDLEY (Alcester)
STURRY (Blean)
SUDBURY (Uttoxeter)
SULGRAVE (Brackley)
SUNBRIDGEWORTH (Bishops
  Stortford)
SUNBURY (Staines)
SUTTON (Chichester)
SUTTON (Ely)
SUTTON (Macclesfield)
SUTTON (Sculcoates)
SUTTON (Thirsk)
SUTTON COLDFIELD (Aston)
SUTTON COURTNEY (Abingdon)
SUTTON IN ASHFIELD (Mansfield)
SWALCLIFFE (Banbury)
SWANAGE (Wareham)
SWAVESLEY (St Ives)
SWINDON (Highworth)
SWINEFLEET (Goole)
SWINESHEAD (Boston)
SYDENHAM (Lewisham)

TALGARTH (Hay)
TALLEY (Llanilofawr)
TALLYLLYN (Dolgelly)
TAMOR (Stoke Damerel)
TANFIELD (Durham)
TANFIELD (Lanchester)
TANWORTH (Solihull)
TARDEBIGG (Bromsgrove)
TARLETON (Ormskirk)
TATTENHALL (Great Boughton)
TATTERSHALL (Horncastle)
TEIGNMOUTH (Newton Abbot)

TENBY (Pembroke)
TERRINGTON ST CLEMENT
  (Wisbech)
TETFORD (Horncastle)
TETNEY (Louth)
TETTENHALL (Wolverhampton)
TEYNHAM (Faversham)
THATCHAM (Newbury)
THAXTED (Dunmow)
THE WORTHYS (Winchester)
THORNABY (Middlesbrough)
THORNEY (Peterborough)
THORNHILL (Dewsbury)
THORNTHWAITE (Pateley Bridge)
THORNTON (Bradford)
THORPE (Tendring)
TICKHILL (Doncaster)
TIDESWELL (Bakewell)
TILEHURST (Bradfield)
TINGEWICK (Buckingham)
TIPTON (Dudley)
TITCHFIELD (Fareham)
TODDINGTON (Woburn)
TOLLESBURY (Maldon)
TONGWITH HAUGH (Bolton)
TOPCLIFFE (Thirsk)
TOPSHAM (St Thomas)
TORBAY (Newton Abbot)
TOTTENHAM (Edmonton)
TOTTINGTON LOWER END (Bury)
TOXTETH PARK (West Derby)
TRANMERE (Birkenhead)
TREDEGAR (Bedwellty)
TRELLECK (Monmouth)
TREMADOC (Festiniog)
TRENTHAM (Stone)
TRING (Berkhamstead)
TROWBRIDGE (Melksham)
TUNBRIDGE WELLS (Tunbridge)
TUNSTAL (Lancaster)
TUNSTALL (Wolstanton)
TURNEY (Bedford)
TURTON (Bolton)
TUTBURY (Burton on Trent)
TUXFORD (East Retford)
TWERTON (Bath)
TWICKENHAM (Brentford)
TWYFORD (Winchester)

UFFCULME (Tiverton)
UGBOROUGH (Totnes)
ULEY (Dursley)
UNY LELANT (Penzance)
UPHOLLAND (Wigan)
UPPER HALLAM (Ecclesall Bierlow)
UPPER MILL (Saddleworth)
UPTON SNODSBURY (Pershore)
UPWAY (Weymouth)
UPWELL (Wisbech)
USK (Pontypool)

WADDESTON (Aylesbury)
WADHURST (Ticehurst)
WALCOT (Bath)
WALL (Church Stretton)
WALLASEY (Birkenhead)
WALLSEND (Tynemouth)
WALMERSLEY (Bury)
WALMGATE (York)
WALPOLE ST PETER (Wisbech)
WALSHAM LE WILLOWS (Stow)
WALSOKEN (Wisbech)
WALTHAM (Melton Mowbray)
WALTHAM ABBEY (Edmonton)
WALTHAMSTOW (West Ham)
WALTON (Brampton)
WALTON (Chertsey)
WALTON (West Derby)
WALTON LE DALE (Preston)
WARBOYS (St Ives)
WARDLEWORTH (Rochdale)
WARGRAVE (Wokingham)
WARKWORTH (Alnwick)
WARSOP (Mansfield)
WASHFIELD (Tiverton)
WASHINGTON (Thakeham)
WATERLOO (Lambeth)
WATH (Ripon)
WATH (Rotherham)
WATLINGTON (Henley)
WATTON (Hertford)
WATTON (Wayland)
WAVERTREE (West Derby)
WEAVERHAM (Northwich)
WEDMORE (Axbridge)
WEEDON (Daventry)
WEEK ST MARY (Stratton)
WELDON (Oundle)

WELLESBOURNE (Stratford on Avon)
WELLS (Walsingham)
WELSHPOOL (Montgomery)
WELWYN (Hatfield)
WENDOVER (Wycombe)
WENDRON (Helston)
WENHASTON (Blything)
WEST ALVINGTON (Kingsbridge)
WEST BROUGHTON (Ulverston)
WEST HOUGHTON (Bolton)
WEST MEON (Droxford)
WEST WYCOMBE (Wycombe)
WEST WYMER (Norwich)
WESTBURY (Atcham)
WESTBURY (Clifton)
WESTFIRLE (Lewes)
WESTGATE (Newcastle upon Tyne)
WESTHAM (Eastbourne)
WESTLEIGH (Leigh)
WESTLETON (Blything)
WESTOE (South Shields)
WESTOW (Malton)
WETHERAL (Carlisle)
WHALLEY (Clitheroe)
WHARTON (Lancaster)
WHEATLEY (Headington)
WHICKHAM (Gateshead)
WHITCHURCH (Cardiff)
WHITCHURCH CANONICORUM (Bridport)
WHITECROSS STREET (St Luke)
WHITFORD (Holywell)
WHITKIRK (Hunslet)
WHITLEY (Pontefract)
WHITMORE (Newcastle under Lyme)
WHITSTABLE (Blean)
WHITWICK (Ashby de la Zouch)
WHITWICK (Barrow on Soar)
WHITWORTH (Rochdale)
WHIXLEY (Great Ouseburn)
WICKFORD (Billericay)
WICKHAM MARKET (Plomesgate)
WICKHAMBROOK (Risbridge)
WIGGENHALL (Downham)
WIGSTON (Blaby)
WILFORD (Basford)
WILHERN (Louth)

WILLENHALL (Wolverhampton)
WILLESDEN (Hendon)
WILLINGHAM (Chesteron)
WILLINGHAM (Gainsbrough)
WILMSLOW (Altrincham)
WILSDEN (Bradford)
WIMBLEDON (Kingston)
WING (Leighton Buzzard)
WINGHAM (Eastry)
WINKLEIGH (Torrington)
WINLATON (Gateshead)
WINTERBOURNE (Amesbury)
WINTERTON (Glanford Bridge)
WINWICK (Warrington)
WIRKSWORTH (Belper)
WITCHAMPTON (Wimborne)
WITHERIDGE (South Molton)
WITHYHAM (East Grinstead)
WITLEY (Hambledon)
WITLEY (Martley)
WITTON (Blackburn)
WIVELSCOMBE (Wellington SOM)
WIVENHOE (Lexden)
WOKING (Guildford)
WOLSINGHAM (Weardale)
WOLVERLEY (Kidderminster)
WOMBOURN (Wolverhampton)
WOMBRIDGE (Wellington SAL)
WOODBURY (St Thomas)
WOODCHURCH (Wirral)
WOODTON (Loddon)
WOOLER (Glendale)
WOOTTON BASSETT (Cricklade)
WOOTTON WAWEN (Stratford on Avon)
WORFIELD (Bridgnorth)
WORKINGTON (Cockermouth)
WORLINGTON (Mildenhall)
WORSBROUGH (Barnsley)
WORSLEY (Barton Irwell)
WORTH (East Grinstead)
WORTLEY (Bramley/Hunslet)
WOTTON UNDER EDGE (Dursley)
WRAGBY (Horncastle)
WRAY (Lancaster/Lunesdale)
WRENBURY (Nantwich)
WRITTLE (Chelmsford)
WROTHAM (Malling)
WUERDLE (Rochdale)

WYBUNBURY (Nantwich)
WYE (East Ashford)
WYKE (Westhampnett)
WYMONDHAM (Forehoe)

YALDING (Maidstone)
YAPTON (Westhampnett)
YARKHILL (Ledbury)
YARM (Stockton)
YATTON (Bedminster)

YEADON (Wharfedale)
YEALMPTON (Plympton St Mary)
YETMINSTER (Sherborne)
YOXALL (Lichfield)
YSPYTTY (Llanrwst)
YSTRADGUNLAIS (Neath)
YSTRADVELLTRY (Neath)
YSTRADYFODWG (Pontypridd)
